# PIPERS FARM

## The Sustainable
## Meat Cookbook

# PIPERS FARM

# The Sustainable Meat Cookbook

## Recipes & Wisdom for Considered Carnivores

**ABBY ALLEN & RACHEL LOVELL**

KYLE BOOKS

This book is dedicated to every hardworking farming family who loves their land and livestock through sheer toil, with hope for a better future for wildlife and rural communities all over the world.

An Hachette UK Company
www.hachette.co.uk

First published in Great Britain in 2022 by
Kyle Books, an imprint of Octopus Publishing Group Ltd
Carmelite House
50 Victoria Embankment
London EC4Y 0DZ

www.kylebooks.co.uk
www.octopusbooksusa.com

ISBN: 978 191423 927 4

Distributed in the US by Hachette Book Group, 1290 Avenue of the Americas,
4th and 5th Floors, New York, NY 10104

Distributed in Canada by Canadian Manda Group, 664 Annette St.,
Toronto, Ontario, Canada M6S 2C8

Publisher: Joanna Copestick
Project Editor: Vicky Orchard
Design: Smith & Gilmour
Photography: Matt Austin
Food & props stylist: Abby Allen
Illustrations: Nicole Heidaripour
Production: Lucy Carter & Nic Jones

A Cataloguing in Publication record for this title is available from the British Library

Printed and bound in China

10 9 8 7 6 5 4 3 2 1

# CONTENTS

# Foreword

The world is waking up to the scale of how the food we choose shapes the world we live in. This is how we must look at the intensive global meat system, which fuels biodiversity loss, deforestation, water pollution and antibiotic resistance. Its impact on society is just as significant, as it erodes our rural economies to the point that the countryside is becoming a playground for the privileged, rather than a green and pleasant patchwork of land cared for by hardworking farming families and brimming with thriving local communities.

But the beautiful part of getting things wrong, is that it brings us closer to getting it right.

Over 30 years ago, Pipers Farm was founded in response to finding myself deep in this dark direction of farming. Like countless other farming families in the 1970s and 80s we were drawn down the path of intensification and scale, and I was farming tens of thousands of chickens in unpleasant sheds in the name of 'progress'. I tried to talk myself down from the constant drumbeat that it just felt wrong, even though everyone said that this was the future of farming. But I knew this was not food I wanted to feed my young family.

I knew there was a better way to produce meat, so my wife Henri and I bought an old farm in a corner of Devon. We brought small herds of native breeds of cattle, sheep and pigs back on to the land, and restored its fertility the natural way. I learned how to seam-butcher our own carcasses, so that every lovingly reared piece of meat could be cooked to perfection and no part of the animal was ever wasted. And I talked, I travelled, I stood up. I took every opportunity I could find to fight for the better way of farming that we believe in, one based on grass, graft and a connection to the land and our animals, not flown-in feed, patented livestock breeds and profit over planet.

As we grew, more farming families joined us, feeding into our system that allows them to concentrate on farming and looking after the countryside, while we butcher and deliver our remarkable meat. This model of direct relationships, with no middleman, is the beating heart of what makes it work. We now count over 40 such farms as part of the Pipers Farm family, and we look after each other.

This would not be possible without our customers, who believe in the better way of farming we stand for. To you I send my deepest thanks. Protecting and sustaining small-scale family farms has myriad ripple effects, bringing jobs, wildlife and community back into our countryside, one life-affirming delivery at a time.

Today the business is led by our son Will and his partner Abby, and Henri and I couldn't be more proud of what we have done together and where we are headed. I believe more fervently than ever that it's time we stop putting our food system in the hands of those who seek short-term gain, and have no respect for nature-friendly farming or the dedicated families who work so hard to care for our countryside. Alongside the beautiful recipes in this book, crafted by the many remarkable cooks who have joined us on our journey, you will also find some deep-rooted wisdom dotted through the pages. These topics cover abattoirs, food waste, animal feed, and native breeds alongside many other food-related issues facing us today. Please read them, share them, talk about them over dinner. Great things can happen when we gather around a table and share good food and grounded wisdom. I invite you to share ours.

**Peter Greig, co-founder of Pipers Farm**

# What on Earth Should We Be Eating?

——

Back in 2013, food campaigner Michael Pollan made a compelling statement that resonates louder than ever today: 'Cooking is a political act'.

His words came in the wake of the horsemeat scandal where ready-meal lasagnes and other processed foods were shown to be loaded with mystery meat alongside an alarming number of artificial ingredients – 60 in the infamous microwaveable 'Rustler' burger. 'When we let corporations cook for us, we lose control. There's an enormous leap of faith to think they are going to have integrity, and that their beef is beef,' he said to the *Independent* at the time.

His point is that by cooking from scratch we control the ingredients that go into our food. This is crucial, as the way in which our food is produced has a staggering impact on our environment, culture, society and communities.

This is a principle that crystallized the forming of Pipers Farm. Large-scale industrialized farming drives climate change, environmental destruction and wildlife loss. It turns food production from a nourishing craft into corporate profiteering that fuels deeply unfair and damaging distribution of wealth.

In contrast, food produced on small-scale family farms using regenerative techniques has the opposite impact. It creates local jobs, keeps money in the rural economy and gives farming families a chance of survival. It encourages biodiversity and enables exceptional standards of care for livestock as farmers can rear native breeds which grow at a natural rate. It minimizes reliance on imported feed and artificial inputs like nitrogen fertilizer, which have huge carbon footprints from their production and destroy soil life, leading to erosion and polluted waterways.

But there's another question at the fore – not just what meat we should be eating, but how much? Should we be eating meat at all? Some believe that a plant-based diet is the best approach for our environment, but we are not convinced. Many ingredients popular in a meat-free diet are imported and grown under environmentally destructive monoculture conditions, requiring artificial fertilizers and biodiversity-depleting pesticides, as well as significant land and water use. The broad-stroke argument that plant-based food is entirely kinder to the environment is deeply flawed. The rise in popularity of plant-based foods has been hijacked by Big Business too, and what you find on the shelves is often ultra-processed food made by those same corporate entities that externalize their costs and have profit at heart.

Our view is that for us to have a hope of tackling the climate and biodiversity crisis, home cooking is crucial - but what we cook needs to change too. We need to embrace a less and better approach to meat. We eat too much in the Western world. By reducing the demand for cheap meat, it removes the economic incentive for factory farming and all its destructive impacts. It allows farmers to rear livestock naturally, with grass under their trotters, feet and hooves, and to be paid fairly for taking care of our countryside. That is our hope, that is the world we are working towards.

Over the years we have shared tips and recipes from our farmhouse table to help you make every piece of meat a treasured, celebrated ingredient that truly shines. You will now find them among the pages of this book. So keep seeking the good meat, the revered meat, keep using every bit you can, waste none, eat it less often and help us build towards that future. We are more determined than ever to make this world a little bit better, through beautiful food, mindfully produced. So here's to less and better meat, produced the Pipers Farm way, with nature, the countryside and communities in mind.

# January

The pleasures to be had in living simply are often the most nourishing, for both body and mind. After the hubbub and perhaps excesses of the festive season, January quietly reminds us to reset and sit with the stillness it brings.

Out on the farm nature is in senescence, and winter finds us cramming as much as we can into each day, before the evenings draw in. Once the animals are tended to, our thoughts turn to the soil, as these are the hours with a little more space for thinking and planning. The farmhouse kitchen remains the refuge, where warming dishes lift the spirits, as we come together over good food.

Venison is such a brilliant ethical meat, it should be celebrated while it's in season. Cooking venison during the darkest winter months not only makes sense for conservation reasons, but it is also incredibly good for you, rich in nutrients that your body is crying out for at this time of year. This recipe is a tonic for the darker days of winter, a fuel to keep you thriving.

# Venison Stew with Bacon & Chestnut Dumplings

— SERVES 4 —

1 tablespoon organic
 rapeseed oil
6 shallots, quartered
2 celery sticks, diced
2 carrots, peeled and diced
150g (5½oz) cep or king oyster
 mushrooms, thickly sliced
250g (9oz) bacon lardons,
 finely chopped
1kg (2lb 4oz) diced venison
5 tablespoons stoneground
 unbleached white flour
2 garlic cloves, finely chopped
1 teaspoon rosemary leaves,
 freshly chopped
2 bay leaves
10 juniper berries,
 lightly crushed
1 orange
400ml (14fl oz) red wine
400ml (14fl oz) beef stock
 (see page 22)
1 tablespoon redcurrant jelly
pure sea salt and freshly
 ground black pepper

*For the dumplings*
150g (5½oz) stoneground
 unbleached white flour
75g (2¾oz) grass-fed beef suet
60g (2¼oz) cooked chestnuts,
 finely chopped
1 teaspoon freshly chopped
 rosemary leaves
about 4 tablespoons
 cold water

Preheat the oven to 160°C/325°F/gas mark 3.

Heat the oil in a large casserole dish. Add the shallots, celery, carrots and mushrooms. Cook over a medium heat for 10–15 minutes until starting to soften and take on a little colour. Remove with a slotted spoon and set aside.

Now, add the bacon and fry for 6–8 minutes until crispy. While the bacon is cooking, season the venison and toss it with the flour to coat it. Remove the crispy bacon with a slotted spoon, keeping as much bacon fat in the pan as possible. Now, add the venison to the pan and fry it in the bacon fat, stirring often, until nicely browned on all sides.

Add the vegetables back into the pan along with half the bacon (keep the other half for the dumplings), the garlic, rosemary, bay leaves, juniper berries and 3 long strips of orange zest. Follow that with the red wine, stock and redcurrant jelly. Use a wooden spoon to scrape and loosen any bits stuck to the base of the pan after browning the meat; it all adds flavour. Bring to a simmer and season with salt and pepper. Pop on a lid and slide it into the oven for 1½ hours.

Just before you take the stew out of oven, make the dumplings. Mix the flour, suet, chestnuts and rosemary together with the reserved bacon in a bowl, then season with salt and pepper, keeping in mind that the bacon will bring some salt to the mix. Stir in the cold water until it just comes together – if it feels too dry, add more water; if a little sticky, then add more flour. Make sure not to overmix, or your dumplings will be heavy and stodgy. Divide into 8 equal balls.

Remove the stew from the oven and arrange the dumplings on top. Return to the oven for 25 minutes until the dumplings are plumped up and lightly coloured on top. The stew should be thickened and glossy and the meat should be completely tender. If it needs longer, pop the lid back on and cook for a further 15 minutes or so.

Serve with plenty of winter greens.

Winter is the ideal time for a warm salad. This dish couldn't get much more filling, and that's before you add any lamb. You don't need much meat – think of it as complementary rather than central to the dish. You could easily use a bit of leftover roast lamb instead, thinly sliced and quickly fried until crispy. Think of the dressing as a grown-up mint sauce, with plenty of briny depth from the capers and anchovies – powerful but perfect.

# Warm Winter Lamb Salad
# with Mint & Anchovy Dressing

— SERVES 2 —

80g (2¾oz) pearled spelt, rinsed
3 medium beetroots
olive oil
2 medium parsnips, peeled
   and cut into chunky batons
1 red onion, cut into wedges
150g (5½oz) cavolo nero,
   leaves stripped and torn
   into bite-sized pieces
a handful of roughly torn
   radicchio or chicory leaves
½ small fennel bulb, thinly sliced
1 pear, very thinly sliced
   lengthways
2 grass-fed lamb steaks
30g (1oz) toasted pine nuts
pure sea salt and freshly
   ground black pepper

*For the dressing*
1 garlic clove
½ tablespoon capers
2 small anchovy fillets
½ tablespoon Dijon mustard
1 tablespoon red wine vinegar
1 small bunch of mint,
   freshly chopped
1 small bunch of flat-leaf
   parsley, freshly chopped
extra virgin olive oil

Boil the kettle and preheat the oven to 200°C/400°F/gas mark 6.

Tip the spelt into a saucepan with a generous pinch of salt and cover with plenty of boiling water. Bring to a simmer and cook for about 45 minutes or until tender. Drain and leave to cool a little.

While the spelt is cooking, give the beets a scrub, rub them with salt and oil and wrap each one in a little parcel of foil. Sit them in a roasting tray, transfer to the oven and roast for 20 minutes.

To make the dressing, put the garlic, capers, anchovies and mustard into a pestle and mortar and smash them together into a paste. Add the vinegar, mint and parsley and continue to work everything together. Add about 3 tablespoons of olive oil, a little at a time, until you have a spoon-able dressing.

Add the parsnips and onion to the beetroots. Lightly oil and season them. Cook for 30 minutes until the parsnips are nicely roasted and the beets are soft to a knife tip. Leave to cool for 10 minutes.

Meanwhile, transfer the cavolo nero to a mixing bowl and add a pinch of salt. Massage the leaves with your hands for a couple of minutes until they darken and soften. Add the radicchio, sliced fennel and pear.

When the beets are cool enough to handle, rub the skins away with your thumbs, trim the tops and cut into wedges.

Heat a drizzle of oil in a frying pan and generously season the lamb. Sear it until nicely coloured on all sides and medium in the middle, this will take about 3–4 minutes for 80g (2¾oz) steaks. Remove them from the pan and leave to rest while you assemble everything.

Tip the spelt and roast veg into the raw ingredients. Tumble them together well and them divide them between 2 plates. Thinly slice the lamb and tuck the slices among the veg. Scatter over the pine nuts before spooning over some dressing to serve.

A great dish doesn't have to be a fancy or complicated affair. Enter beans on toast. As a nation, the UK has been fascinated with beans on toast ever since Mr Heinz brought his shiny turquoise cans into our kitchens in 1886. However, there are as many as eight cubes of sugar lurking in one can of ready-made baked beans! Baked beans are also fiendishly simple to make, and the homemade version is much more rewarding to eat. Far, far greater than the sum of its parts, the combination of haricot beans, bacon and trotters is rich, complex and satisfying. Pork's natural affinity with beans of any sort can be something to take advantage of here. You could use haricot or carlin, even chickpeas, or chunks of chorizo instead of the bacon.

# Bacon & Trotter Baked Beans

## — SERVES 2 —

olive oil
250g (9oz) bacon lardons
1 onion, diced
400g (14oz) can chopped
   tomatoes
2 tablespoons balsamic vinegar
5 garlic cloves, 3 finely sliced
   and 2 bashed  (optional)
3 bay leaves, plus extra if
   using dried beans
3 large sprigs of thyme
2 pig's trotters
150g (5½oz) dried borlotti
   beans, soaked overnight,
   or 400g (14oz) can
   borlotti beans
pure sea salt and freshly
   ground black pepper

Preheat the oven to 150°C/300°F/gas mark 2.

Place a casserole dish over a high heat, add a drizzle of olive oil and fry off the bacon lardons until golden and crispy. Add the onion and gently cook for about 8 minutes until soft and translucent.

Add the tomatoes, along with the balsamic vinegar, sliced garlic, bay leaves and thyme. Half-fill the empty tomatoes can with water and pour in. Add the trotters to the dish, pop the lid on and cook in the oven for 3 hours.

If you are using the soaked beans, place them in a large saucepan and cover them with 3 times the volume of water. Add a couple of extra bay leaves and the bashed garlic cloves and season well. Bring to the boil and immediately reduce the heat to a gentle simmer. Cook for 45 minutes–1 hour until creamy and tender. Drain and dress with olive oil, cover and set to one side. If using canned beans, drain thoroughly.

Remove the casserole dish from the oven. Remove the trotters from the dish and pick off all the meat and gelatinous skin, dice it all up and return to the casserole dish. Add the beans and stir to combine. Bring the whole dish to a simmer. Season with salt and plenty of pepper.

Serve with buttered sourdough toast.

# How to Make
# Chicken Stock & Beef Stock

—

Incorporating stock-making into your routine means you'll waste less food and get better value from your ingredients by using up every last morsel. Making a proper stock honours the life of the animal, by paying respect to every single ounce of protein and never wasting any part. What's more, it is also packed full of vitamins and minerals that will help you to ward off winter colds.

Without a healthy gut, your body will not be able to properly digest and absorb vital vitamins and minerals. Even if you are eating wholesome and nourishing foods, you may not be reaping all the benefits. A good chicken or beef stock is an excellent foundation to help heal, soothe and protect your gut.

It goes without saying, to produce the healthiest, tastiest stock you must use ingredients from healthy animals. Only properly free-ranging livestock will build up real collagen, marrow and gelatine by forming a strong carcass from all their running around. Free-ranging, purely grass-fed animals will also pick up vitamins and minerals from their varied diet, and access to long periods of sunlight creates superior levels of CLA (conjugated linoleic acids). UV light also suppresses bad bacteria, allowing cattle and chickens to develop natural immunity which is stored within the memory bank of their marrow.

# How to Make Chicken Stock

There is no bigger crime than to roast a whole chicken and not make a stock afterwards. A proper chicken stock has to be one of our most prized pantry ingredients; it holds the key to so many delicious dishes to come. You don't just have to wait until you roast a chicken to fill your freezer with nutrient-rich stock, chicken stock can be made from scratch using just a few really low-cost ingredients.

2 free-range chicken carcasses
250g (9oz) free-range chicken
   wings (plus feet and necks
   of chicken, if you have
   access to them)
4 bay leaves
a handful of garden herbs
   (we like thyme and leftover
   parsley stalks)
any leftover veg peelings
   (onion skins, carrots,
   leek ends are all perfect)
a few black peppercorns

Preheat the oven to 140°C/275°F/gas mark 1.

Take a lidded, ovenproof dish and place the chicken carcasses, wings, herbs, vegetable peelings and peppercorns into the base. Fill with water until all of your ingredients are submerged.

Take a sheet of greaseproof paper and measure the diameter of your pot, then cut a circle with a small overlap to make a 'cartouche'. A cartouche is a lid that allows for some evaporation during slow cooking while keeping the meat submerged. Place the cartouche on the top of the liquid-filled pan and pop the lid on.

Place the dish into the oven and leave to cook, depending on your desired intent for the stock. If you are looking to make a simple base for another meal such as a soup, a 2-hour cooking time will suffice. If your intent is to make a nutritious sipping broth, you'll need to aim for at least 4 hours. For a super intense gelatine, reminiscent of a jellied stock cube, you'll need to cook your stock for 8–12 hours.

Remove the dish from the oven and pour the stock through a sieve. Your stock can be poured into sterilized jam jars and kept in the fridge for a week, or poured into Tupperware containers and frozen to use another day.

## How to Make Beef Stock

The best way to make beef stock is to cook it gently for a very long time. This creates a gelatinous, highly concentrated stock that can be brought to life and liquid form just by heating, or spooned from its container and added to another recipe you may have on the go (think cottage pies, bolognese or beef stew) to add a punch of flavour and nutrients.

1kg (2lb 4oz) grass-fed
    beef bones
750g (1lb 10oz) grass-fed oxtail
3 medium onions, skin on
    and halved
3 carrots, skin on and
    chopped into 3 chunks
2 garlic cloves, skin on
10 bay leaves
a few sprigs of thyme
a few parsley stalks
1 teaspoon black peppercorns

Preheat the oven to 140°C/275°F/gas mark 1.

Take a lidded, ovenproof dish and place the beef bones, oxtail, vegetables, garlic, herbs and peppercorns into the base. Fill with water until all of your ingredients are submerged.

Take a sheet of greaseproof paper and measure the diameter of your pot, then cut a circle with a small overlap to make a 'cartouche'. A cartouche is a lid that allows for some evaporation during slow cooking while keeping the meat submerged. Place the cartouche on the top of the liquid-filled pan and pop the lid on.

Place the dish into the oven and leave to cook for 8–10 hours or overnight if possible.

Remove the dish from the oven and pour the stock through a sieve. Your stock can be poured into sterilized jam jars and kept in the fridge for a week, or poured into Tupperware containers and frozen to use another day.

A meal for four with two chicken thighs sounds like a big ask, but it is more than possible alongside the earthy lentils, proper stock and some stout winter veg. Shred the meat well and you won't believe how little you need for a generous bowlful. The gremolata smash is the perfect condiment – pungent from the garlic and bitter walnuts but with an uplifting zing from the lemon and fresh parsley.

# Chicken & Lentil Stew
# with Walnut Gremolata Smash

## — SERVES 4 —

2 tablespoons organic
   rapeseed oil
2 properly free-range
   chicken thighs
2 carrots, peeled and finely diced
2 celery sticks, finely diced
2 leeks, thinly sliced
½ tablespoon thyme leaves
1 sprig of rosemary,
   freshly chopped
1 bay leaf
200ml (7fl oz) white wine
1 litre (1¾ pints) chicken
   stock (see page 21)
½ celeriac, peeled and diced
130g (4½oz) green lentils,
   rinsed (we like Hodmedod's)
150g (5½oz) cavolo nero,
   roughly shredded
pure sea salt and freshly
   ground black pepper

*For the walnut gremolata smash*
zest of 1 lemon, plus juice for
   the stew
1 garlic clove, finely chopped
1 bunch of flat-leaf parsley,
   finely chopped
40g (1½oz) walnuts
2 tablespoons extra virgin
   olive oil

Heat 1 tablespoon of the oil in a large flameproof casserole dish or saucepan. Season the chicken thighs with salt and pepper and brown them on both sides over a medium heat. Remove the chicken to a plate.

Keep the dish over the heat and add the carrots, celery and leeks, along with the remaining tablespoon of oil. Cook over a gentle heat for about 5 minutes until starting to soften. Stir often and use the spoon to scrape and loosen anything left from frying the chicken.

Add the thyme, rosemary and bay leaf to the pan. Cook for 2 minutes, then pour in the wine. Increase the heat and let the wine bubble and reduce by half before tipping in the stock and returning the chicken thighs to the pan. Season with salt and pepper and bring to a gentle simmer. Cook gently for 15 minutes.

Add the celeriac and lentils to the pan and continue to gently simmer for about 25 minutes until the lentils are just cooked and the chicken is tender. Lift the chicken out of the pan and set aside. Stir in the cavolo nero and simmer gently for a final 5 minutes before turning off the heat, popping on a lid and leaving it to stand for 10–15 minutes while you prepare the chicken and gremolata smash.

Add the lemon zest, garlic and parsley to a pestle and mortar along with the walnuts and a pinch of salt. Smash it all together into a coarse paste and then stir in the olive oil, adding enough to give you a pesto-like consistency.

Remove and discard the skin from the chicken and pull the meat away from the bones. Shred the meat with your fingertips. Stir the meat back into the dish. Taste and tweak the seasoning with salt, pepper and a squeeze or two of lemon juice, to suit your taste. Remove the bay leaf. Serve in bowls, finished with a spoonful of the walnut gremolata smash.

Our grass-fed lamb neck is the ideal cut of meat for low and slow cooking, as the marbling releases an abundance of flavour when melted. The rich, deep lamby flavour is balanced by the fresh sweetness of the tangy salsa verde. Comforting and warming, this dish is perfect for sheltering from the elements on a cosy night in, giving your body a much-needed boost of vitamins from the nutrient-rich ingredients.

# Lamb Neck Broth with Kale, Spelt & Salsa Verde

— SERVES 4 —

organic rapeseed oil
1 grass-fed lamb's neck,
    cut into 2.5cm (1in) cubes
400g (14oz) can chopped
    tomatoes
60g (2¼oz) pearled spelt
juice of ½ lemon, plus extra
    for the salsa verde if needed
1 small bunch of kale, such
    as cavolo nero

*For the salsa verde*
1 small bunch of
    flat-leaf parsley
1 garlic clove
4 anchovy fillets
1 teaspoon Dijon mustard
3 tablespoons extra virgin
    olive oil, plus extra
    for drizzling
a pinch of sea salt
a pinch of freshly ground
    black pepper

Preheat the oven to 140°C/275°F/gas mark 1.

Heat a heavy-based frying pan over a high heat, add a little oil and cook the diced lamb until beautifully browned. Depending on the size of your frying pan, you may need to cook the meat in several batches to avoid overcrowding the pan. Transfer the browned lamb to a deep, ovenproof casserole dish. Add the tomatoes, spelt, lemon juice and a couple of glasses of water. Cover with a lid or some foil and place in the oven for 3 hours or until the spelt is fully cooked.

While the lamb is cooking, prepare the salsa verde. Finely chop the parsley and transfer to a small mixing bowl. Grate the clove of garlic and finely chop the anchovies and add to the parsley. Add the mustard, olive oil, salt and pepper. Stir to combine and check for seasoning, adjusting with lemon juice as required.

Taste the lamb broth and season if necessary. Finely slice the kale and stir through the lamb broth until it wilts and becomes tender. Serve in bowls with a drizzle of olive oil and some good bread.

Haggis is not only really delicious, but it's also really good for you as it's packed full of vitamins and nutrients. One of the main ingredients of haggis is liver, which is high in vitamin A, vitamin B12 and folate. If you're intrigued by haggis, our delicious, all-natural recipe is a million miles from the mass-produced novelty versions you'll find on the supermarket shelves.

# Haggis

— SERVES 8 —

1 ox bung
300g (10½oz) lamb's liver, diced
300g (10½oz) Saddleback pig's liver, diced
150g (5½oz) lamb's heart, diced
150g (5½oz) Saddleback pig's heart, diced
400g (14oz) diced lamb
400g (14oz) grass-fed beef suet
300g (10½oz) organic rolled oats
25g (1oz) pure sea salt
12g (½oz) black pepper
10g (¼oz) garden herbs, such as sage and rosemary, freshly chopped
10g (¼oz) coriander seeds, ground
10g (¼oz) mace

Wash the bung and soak it in a bowl of cold water for 24 hours. Be careful how you handle the bung as you do not want to pierce the skin.

Mix the offal with the diced lamb, suet and oats. To the meat add the seasonings; salt, pepper, chopped garden herbs, coriander and mace, and mix together. Put the mixture through a mincer and, using a coarse blade, mince through just once. If you don't have a mincer, simply finely dice the meat (we do recommend using a mincer, if possible).

Give the meat a quick knead to ensure that it's thoroughly mixed.

Cut the ox bung in half. Take an end and tie a tight knot in it with some string.

Carefully spoon half the meat mixture into the ox bung, don't pack it too tightly or there's a risk of it bursting when cooking. You will end up with a slightly soft, oval-shaped ball. Tie the haggis off at the other end as tightly as you can, leaving 2.5cm (1in) of skin at either end.

Repeat for the second haggis.

To cook, place both haggis into a pan of gently simmering (not boiling) water and cook very gently for 2 hours, being careful not to allow it to boil as this could split the ox bung. You may have to top up the water during this time.

To serve the haggis, slice through the skin and spoon out the meat and serve with mashed swede and parsnip, gravy and buttered greens.

# February

Life in the countryside seems to have all but frozen. Real sustenance is required to nourish and revive after biting cold days and relentless grey skies. Yet the snowdrops push through the seemingly fervourless soil, reminding us of the power of nature. This is the time for digging deep and sitting with our thoughts, reading by the fire, and taking time in the kitchen over slow-cooking dishes and gently blipping pans.

It is tempting to hibernate like the bats in the barn, and wait for spring's gentle awakening, but there are jobs to be done; fences to mend, frozen drinking water to thaw, sheep to move and plans to be put into action to set us up for the year ahead.

This is the perfect recipe for a long winter weekend, when you have time at home to slow down the pace of life and immerse yourself in the joys of a gentler, more natural way of living. There are plenty of ways you can cook a mutton shoulder, but we love this 'all in one pan' approach, with chickpeas, garlic, chilli and plenty of spice to liven up a cold, grey day.

# Slow-roast Shoulder of Mutton with Chickpeas, Orange, Cumin & Garlic

## — SERVES 6 —

2.5kg (5lb 8oz) grass-fed mutton shoulder
2 tablespoons extra virgin olive oil
2 onions, finely sliced
350g (12oz) dried chickpeas, soaked overnight (we like Hodmedod's)
500ml (18fl oz) beef stock (see page 22)
6 garlic cloves, finely sliced
1 medium-hot chilli, thinly sliced
3 teaspoons cumin seeds, toasted and crushed
3 teaspoons coriander seeds, toasted and crushed
1 teaspoon fenugreek seeds, toasted and crushed
zest and juice 1 orange
4 sprigs of rosemary
1 bunch of flat-leaf parsley, freshly chopped
pure sea salt and freshly ground black pepper

Preheat the oven to 200°C/400°F/gas mark 6.

Sit the mutton shoulder in a large, deep roasting tray. Trickle over half the olive oil and season generously with salt and pepper. Cook in the oven for 20–30 minutes so that it takes on some colour.

Pour the remaining oil into a saucepan, add the onions, season with a little salt and pepper, then cook, stirring occasionally, for about 6 minutes until they are beginning to soften and smell amazing. Add the drained chickpeas and cook them with the onions for a further 5 minutes. Add the stock and bring to a gentle simmer.

Remove the roasting tray from the oven and lift the mutton shoulder out on to a plate. Now add the chickpea mixture to the roasting tray along with the garlic, chilli, spices, orange zest and rosemary sprigs. Season with salt and pepper, give the tray a shake to even them all out, then place the mutton back in. Cover the tray with foil or baking parchment – this will help to seal in all the steam as the meat cooks.

Reduce the oven temperature to 150°C/300°F/gas mark 2, set the tray in the middle of the oven and cook slowly for 4–5 hours. To test if the meat is cooked, lift away the foil and make sure the meat is coming away from the bone. It should be fork tender. Scatter over the freshly chopped flat-leaf parsley and drizzle over the orange juice. Taste and adjust the seasoning if required.

Serve with a sharply dressed salad.

Like pasta, there is a perception that noodles are difficult to make at home. We're here to tell you that this is simply not the case! Just three ingredients and a bit of TLC is all that you need to make these wholesome and healthy noodles. It might seem daunting to make these strands of goodness from scratch, but do it once and you'll want to do it all the time.

# Homemade Noodles with Crispy Lamb & Cumin Stir-fry

— SERVES 2 —

### For the noodles

200g (7oz) stoneground unbleached white flour, plus extra for dusting
2 free-range and/or organic eggs
1 tablespoon miso paste (we like Hodmedod's Fava Bean Umami Paste)
pure sea salt

### For the stir-fry

200g (7oz) leftover roast lamb shoulder, shredded
½ onion, chopped
2 garlic cloves, chopped
a small knob of fresh ginger, peeled and chopped
1 chilli, deseeded and chopped
2 tablespoons ground cumin
2 tablespoons miso paste
1 tablespoon chilli flakes
a handful of pumpkin seeds
1 small bunch of green beans, shredded
1 small bunch of coriander, roughly chopped
juice of 1 lime

Add the flour, eggs and miso paste to a mixing bowl and mix together until you have formed a dough. Knead the dough for 10 minutes until it has become smooth and glossy, then wrap in clingfilm or beeswax wraps and leave to rest in the fridge for 2 hours.

Once 2 hours is up, roll out the dough on a floured surface. You want to roll it really thin, about 1mm (1⁄32in). Once rolled out, slice the dough into 3mm (1⁄8in) wide strips.

Pour some boiling water into a pan and season with a generous pinch of salt. Blanch the noodles in the boiling water for 1 minute. Then remove the noodles from the water, holding back a little of the starchy cooking water for later.

In a frying pan, sauté the lamb for 6 minutes until golden and crispy. Add the onion, garlic, ginger and chilli and sweat down for a couple of minutes. Add the cumin, miso paste and chilli flakes and cook for a further few minutes to allow the flavours to infuse through the meat. Then add the pumpkin seeds and green beans and stir well. Finally, add the noodles along with a couple of tablespoons of the cooking water. Like pasta, the cooking water is essential to help the flavours combine well and encourages the silky sauce to stick to the noodles.

Finish with a generous scattering of freshly chopped coriander and a squeeze of lime juice.

# From Food Waste to Cooking Flow

---

It wasn't that long ago that we cooked in a very different way. Cooking started with the question 'What do I have?', rather than 'What do I want?' In a 1950s, 60s or even 70s kitchen, meals began with the pocket and the pantry as they had for centuries before, and for a wartime kitchen, rations ruled. With the arrival of convenience food alongside stretched time, lost kitchen skills, and the bombardment of ads and delivery apps making seductive food instant at every turn, the time built into the day for meal preparation has drifted away. Somehow thoughts turn to food when hunger strikes, rather than to cooking an hour earlier, like it is a surprise to find that we need to get something on the table. This creeping evolution towards instant food is damaging in many ways. It costs far more than cooking from scratch and widens the gap between people and where their food comes from. This opacity around the story of ingredients, where no-one is held to account, creates space for supply chain corruption and means animal welfare and environmental impact don't even appear on the scorecard. Takeaways are about flavour and trends, not responsibility and impact.

It's how food waste is fuelled too. Forgotten ingredients wither in the fridge when we reach for food without taking a moment to think, whether we're ordering on an app or making a supermarket pit stop. This issue is magnified when we put what we spend on food in context. For most, it is the biggest expense after our mortgage or rent. Just five minutes a week of planning can create a revolution in our kitchens, from our bank balances to our planet. The farming system we support through our food choices has a staggering impact on the planet's

health. At the other end of the food chain, what we do with that food plays a big part too.

This doesn't mean we must stop enjoying delicious food; instead eating needs to be led largely by the contents of a considered storecupboard rather than the stomach. A philosophy based on seasonality feels like it may have gotten a bit trendy, but the reality is that this is the best way – for our planet, pocket and sanity. It is the philosophy of planning and cooking flow that we need to restore, where eating is mapped out and each meal leads to the next, rather than starting over each time. Working family farmhouses may be increasingly rare, but the culinary approach is rooted in a timeless sense and sensibility (the kind without knee breeches and frilly dresses). Traditionally, a constant flow of family and farmworkers would need feeding, hungry from physical work, and the cooking would be centred around an endless series of harvests, both great and small. A killed pig meant offal first, the fastest to perish, and with its strong flavour it could be stretched across weeks of dishes if carefully preserved and handled. Bacon and ham would be salted, preserved and crafted and the prime cuts would be frozen, to come out perhaps once or twice a month as a special roast, and nose to tail, the rest would be prized and worked through.

Woven alongside each meat harvest would be the everyday work of the kitchen garden, where seasonal vegetables could really take centre stage. Meat was treated as a seasoning, as slowly grown species are loaded with flavour in a way that intensively farmed, rapidly grown meat is not. Pulses and potatoes, leafy greens and earthy roots are wonderful vehicles for all that taste. Any bones were picked of meat and

*This is the opposite of Instagram cooking. It's an interior journey, a mental mini-break with added nutrition, designed to inspire not impress.*

boiled up for stock. The fat from the cuts and carcass slowly rendered down and stored for future cooking and layering more meaty notes. Leftovers from yesterday started the thoughts of food for today.

While a typical household can't be expected to mirror a working farmhouse kitchen, the principles of connecting our cooking across days, weeks and months and using every part of the animal can be revived. This thoughtful, considered whole-kitchen approach brings with it added benefits for our ever-frazzled minds too. Cooking can be a kind of meditation; the chop-chop-chop, the sizzle and turn of the pan perhaps alongside something easy-going on the radio. For many, it is one of the few opportunities we get to do something with our hands, and both cooking and eating provide a mental mini-break in our ever-crowded heads and schedules. It is also because cooking is a feeling. It's about meeting a human need for nourishment and hunger, yes, but it is as much about emotion as sensation.

This is the opposite of Instagram cooking. It's an interior journey, a mental mini-break with added nutrition, designed to inspire not impress. This is cooking with no Aga required; everyone can embrace it. It's not about the kitchen fittings, it's about kitchen philosophy.

So less and better meat, mindfully cooked, in a kitchen connected across dishes, days and dinnertimes, for everyone. Back to a better way.

# How to Make Salt Beef

With a little patience, you can take an often overlooked cut and turn it into something so mouthwateringly delicious, that you'll be finding excuse after excuse to visit the fridge. Salt beef makes the perfect sandwich filling or cold cut that keeps you going all week when life is hectic and you need something tasty to grab and go.

**SERVES 8**

2kg (4lb 8oz) beef brisket
1 onion, chopped
2 carrots, peeled and chopped
½ garlic bulb, sliced horizontally
8 bay leaves

*For the brine*
2.5 litres (4½ pints) water
500g (1lb 2oz) fine salt
300g (10½oz) dark brown sugar
6 bay leaves
4 sprigs of rosemary
2 tablespoons fennel seeds
2 garlic cloves, bashed

Combine all the brine ingredients in a saucepan and bring to a simmer, this will allow the salt and sugar to dissolve and all the flavours to combine. Remove from the heat and leave to cool to room temperature.

Put the brisket in a large plastic container. Coat the brisket with the brining mixture, thoroughly rubbing it into the meat and any surrounding fat. Make sure your brisket is well covered with liquid and then pop in the fridge and leave to cure for 2 days.

Remove the brisket from the brine and pour away the cure. Using some kitchen paper, pat the beef dry and leave it to properly dry out for 2–3 hours.

Throw the chopped onion and carrots, garlic and bay leaves into a large pot. Add the brisket and pour over a generous covering of water. Bring to the boil, then turn down the heat and gently simmer the brisket for 2–3 hours (depending on the thickness). This breaks down the collagen in the meat, turning it into gelatin, resulting in the juicy texture you want for great salt beef. Cook for a further hour if you prefer the salt beef to be almost falling apart when you bite into it.

Remove the pan from the heat and leave the salt beef to cool for 30 minutes, then lift it out on to a chopping board (use the leftover broth as the base for a soup, if you like). Slice the salt beef thickly and load straight into bagels while still warm or make our utterly delicious Reuben-style Sandwiches with Homemade Sauerkraut on the next page.

Turn your home into a New-York-style deli with this delicious, leftover-loving feast! Start with the leftovers from our homemade salt beef; add a heap of homemade tangy sauerkraut, then load as many pickles as you can into this classic sandwich.

# Reuben-style Sandwiches with Homemade Sauerkraut

## — SERVES 4 —

*For the sauerkraut*
2.5kg (5lb 8oz) white cabbage, any old outer leaves removed
5 tablespoons coarse pure sea salt
2 teaspoons caraway seeds

*For the sandwich*
a knob of grass-fed butter
8 slices of rye bread
1–2 teaspoons English mustard
300g (10½oz) leftover salt beef, thinly sliced (see page 40)
a few gherkins or pickled cucumber slices
200g (7oz) sauerkraut, plus extra to serve
200g (7oz) clothbound mature or vintage Cheddar, sliced

*You will need*
2-litre (3½-pint) sterilized jar with a lid
1 plastic freezer bag
1 clean airtight container

Cut the cabbage into quarters, removing the tough core. Slice across the cabbage as thinly as possible to create shredded leaves. Place the shredded cabbage into a mixing bowl and pour over the salt and caraway seeds.

Massage the salt and seeds into the cabbage, pushing down as you massage to allow the salt to break up the leaves. You'll need to do this quite intensely for 5–6 minutes. Cover the bowl with a clean tea towel and then repeat the massaging process again in an hour.

After you have completed the second massaging of the cabbage leaves, you should notice quite a lot of liquid has been drawn out of the cabbage. Pour this into the sterilized jar, then tightly pack the cabbage in, making sure there are no gaps between the shredded leaves. The brine should cover the top of the cabbage leaves. You'll need to push the cabbage down into the jar using a weight. Take the plastic freezer bag and fill it up to about halfway with water and tie a knot in the top, then place this in the top of the jar. Leave the lid open and keep the jar at room temperature out of direct sunlight for at least 5 days. For maximum flavour, leave the cabbage to ferment for up to 2 weeks (or until the bubbling subsides, if you dare). Once you are happy with the fermented flavour, decant the cabbage into a clean airtight container and store it in the fridge. It will keep in the fridge for about a month.

Preheat the oven to 190°C/375°F/gas mark 5.

Butter the rye bread and slather both buttered sides generously with mustard. On one slice, layer the sliced salt beef on top of the mustard, place a couple of gherkins on top, then add the sauerkraut and finish with the Cheddar. Place the other slice of bread on top and transfer to a tray lined with greaseproof paper. Repeat with the remaining slices of bread and filling. Cook the sandwiches for 5–6 minutes, turning halfway through cooking, until the rye bread is lightly toasted and the cheese has melted.

Serve with extra pickles and sauerkraut.

As the saying goes, 'Cooking is like love: It should be entered into with abandon or not at all'. What's better than showing someone you love them by cooking a thoughtful, delicious meal? This is the recipe you need up your sleeve when Valentine's Day rolls around.

# Côte de Boeuf with Dauphinoise Potatoes

— SERVES 2 —

1 côte de boeuf
olive oil
50g (1¾oz) salted
    grass-fed butter
2 garlic cloves, bashed
1 small bunch of thyme

*For the dauphinoise potatoes*
200ml (7fl oz) double cream
2 garlic cloves, grated
1 tablespoon finely
    chopped thyme
¼ bulb of nutmeg, grated
375g (13oz) waxy potatoes,
    peeled and finely sliced
grass-fed butter, for greasing
pure sea salt and freshly
    ground black pepper

Preheat the oven to 180°C/350°F/gas mark 4. Remove the côte de boeuf from the fridge an hour before you plan on cooking it to bring it up to room temperature. Season well with salt and pepper.

To make the dauphinoise, warm the cream in a small saucepan with the garlic, thyme and nutmeg. Season this cream really well with salt and pepper. It's important to get it almost over seasoned, as it will have the job of seasoning the potatoes as well. Place the potatoes in a bowl, pour over the cream and mix thoroughly.

Grease a small baking dish with butter. Layer up the potatoes in the dish until it's full. Place a sheet of baking parchment over the surface of the potatoes and bake for 25 minutes. Remove the baking parchment and return the dish to the oven for a further 15 minutes until the top of the dauphinoise takes on some colour.

Heat a wide, heavy-based frying until hot. Add a drizzle of oil to the outside of the côte de boeuf and place in the pan, fat-side down. Use a pair of tongs to hold the piece of beef in place and carefully render down the fat, creating a lovely golden crust on the beef fat.

Remove the beef from the pan and pour away any excess fat. Increase the heat of the pan until very hot, then add the beef, cut-side down, and fiercely sear the meat for 2 minutes on each side.

Once again remove the beef from the pan and leave the pan to cool a little. Now add the butter, bashed garlic and sprigs of thyme to create an aromatic butter. Return the beef to the pan and continue to cook on each side. It is useful at this stage to have a digital temperature probe to keep track of how the beef is cooking. For rare, aim for a core temperature of 48–52°C (118–126°F); for medium aim for 55–58°C (131–136°F) and 60°C+ (140°F+) for well done. If you don't have a temperature probe, cooking the beef in the butter for a further 4 minutes on each side should work well.

Transfer the beef to a tray, pour over the butter and leave to rest for 10 minutes. Carve into thick slices and serve with the rich dauphinoise potatoes and a sharp watercress salad.

Bitter radicchio, sweet beetroot, rich duck and salty cheese, this rather fine warm salad just about covers every flavour sensation you can imagine. Packed full of essential vitamins and minerals, a little of this impressive salad goes a long way.

# Warm Salad of Duck, Radicchio, Beetroot & Stilton

## — SERVES 4 —

a large bunch of young
    beetroots
olive oil
2 heads of radicchio,
    cut into wedges
1 tablespoon balsamic
    vinegar
2 duck breasts
1 sprig of sage
a knob of grass-fed butter
a small handful of
    walnuts
1 small bunch of thyme,
    leaves picked
100g (3½oz) Stilton cheese
    (we like Cropwell Bishop)
pure sea salt and freshly
    ground black pepper

Preheat the oven to 180°C/350°F/gas mark 4.

Cut the beetroots into wedges and dress with olive oil and salt. Place on a baking tray and roast in the oven for 15 minutes.

Remove the beetroots from the oven and add the radicchio wedges, mix together with the beetroots and place back into the oven to roast for a further 10 minutes. Remove from the oven and stir in the balsamic vinegar. Set aside while you prepare the duck.

Season the duck breasts and then place them in a hot frying pan. Caramelize the duck breasts, skin-side down, for about 4 minutes. Turn the breasts over and cook for a further 5 minutes. Then add the sage and the butter to the pan. Baste the duck breasts for a further 5 minutes. Remove the duck from the pan and leave to rest for 5–10 minutes.

In a separate pan, toast the walnuts with a little olive oil and the thyme. Lightly crush the walnuts to release their nutty savoury aroma.

Cut the duck breasts into thick slices. Combine the duck, beetroots, raddichio and walnuts together, then crumble the Stilton over the top.

The veg garden can often look a little uninspiring in February. You may have had root veg overload and be craving something green and iron-rich. Enter seasonal star purple sprouting broccoli, the saviour of the British 'hungry gap'. Buttery, rich pork neck steaks pair wonderfully with this slightly bitter brassica.

# Pork Steaks with Purple Sprouting Broccoli, Almonds & Yogurt

— SERVES 2–3 —

300g (10½oz) purple sprouting broccoli
olive oil
2 pork neck steaks
50g (1¾oz) salted grass-fed butter, melted
1 teaspoon freshly chopped thyme
100g (3½oz) yogurt, seasoned with pure sea salt
50g (1¾oz) roasted almonds, roughly chopped
1 teaspoon smoked paprika
juice of ½ lemon
pure sea salt and freshly ground black pepper

Bring a medium pan of water to the boil and blanch the broccoli for 1 minute, then drain.

Preheat a heavy-based griddle pan until scorchingly hot. Season the broccoli with salt and pepper and drizzle with olive oil. Add the broccoli to the pan and cook for 2 minutes on each side so that it takes on a good level of smokiness. Set to one side on a large platter.

Season the pork with salt and drizzle with olive oil. Cook for 3–4 minutes on each side, then set aside to rest in the melted butter with the chopped thyme for 5 minutes.

Slice the pork steak into 1cm (½in) slices and arrange around the griddled broccoli. Dot the yogurt around the broccoli, scatter with the almonds, smoked paprika and the lemon juice. Serve with good bread.

There is something rather medieval about oxtail. The gnarly, bony joints might not look like much, but those in the know are all too aware of the hidden magic that is kept within this old-fashioned cut. All it needs is time. Time to release the heavenly marrow that slowly marinates the dish. Time to allow the tough sinews to relax and relent, leaving you with flakes of beefy delight. This is proper hearty food that packs a punch. The perfect fodder for chilly evenings, when only something warming and eaten with a spoon will do.

# Oxtail Ragù with Rigatoni

— SERVES 3–4 —

1kg (2lb 4oz) ripe tomatoes
olive oil
2 tablespoons grass-fed
    beef dripping
500g (1lb 2oz) grass-fed
    beef oxtail
2 white onions, diced
8 garlic cloves, crushed
1 fennel bulb, finely sliced
3 celery sticks, diced
2 sprigs of rosemary
5 bay leaves
375ml (13fl oz) red wine
1 litre (1¾ pints) beef stock
    (see page 22)
500g (1lb 2oz) cooked
    rigatoni
pure sea salt

Preheat the oven to 180°C/350°F/gas mark 4.

While the oven is preheating, roughly chop the tomatoes and mix with a little olive oil and salt. Spread them out over a tray and then roast for about 20 minutes until they are completely juicy and soft.

Next, heat a large, heavy-based ovenproof saucepan with the beef dripping. Add the oxtail to the pan and caramelize it in the beef dripping for about 5 minutes until golden brown. Remove the oxtail from the pan and set aside.

Add the onions and garlic to the same pan and sweat for 5 minutes. Add the fennel, celery and the herbs and cook for a further 5 minutes, mixing it all together. Return the oxtail to the pan, followed by the wine and the stock. Let the oxtail, veggies and liquid blip away on the hob over a low heat until it has reduced by half. Once this has happened, add the cooked tomatoes into the pan.

At this point, pop on the lid and place the whole pan in the oven for 3½ hours at 160°C/325°F/gas mark 3 or until the meat is falling off the bone. After this, the bones can be pulled out.

To serve, add the pasta, stir everything together and grab a fork. No plates needed; this dish is designed to be devoured straight away!

# March

Around mid-March comes a day or two when you can smell spring easing in on the wind. The soil has been ticking over but now she's starting her engines as temperatures lift and the sap starts to rise. Crucially, at 6°C (43°F) the grass starts to grow again – the magic of this renewal of life never ceases to stir spirits and lift our thoughts.

This fresh arrival of nutritious first growth is perfect for lactating mothers too, and we see cattle calving, we tend to our lambing ewes in the soft spring nights, and watch the pigs collect mouthfuls of grass and straw as they build their nests ready for farrowing.

Cooking in hay may seem like a new food trend, but it has actually been around for centuries. It's the marriage of the animal with the food it was reared on, and the two sit sublimely together in perfect harmony. The hay infuses the meat with an earthy, bonfire fragrance, gently smoking the mutton while keeping it beautifully tender.

# Roast Mutton Cooked in Hay with Baked Potatoes, Garlic & Green Herb Sauce

— SERVES 6 —

1 leg of mutton on the bone
2 tablespoons olive oil
6 medium baking potatoes
3 bulbs of garlic, halved
a couple of handfuls of wild meadow hay (optional)
pure sea salt and freshly ground black pepper

*For the green herb sauce*
a handful of flat-leaf parsley, leaves picked
a small handful of mint
1 tablespoon capers
2 tablespoons Dijon mustard
1 small garlic clove, grated
1 tablespoon cider vinegar
3 tablespoons extra virgin olive oil, plus extra to loosen (if necessary)

Preheat the oven to 200°C/400°F/gas mark 6.

Place the mutton leg in a large roasting tray and rub it all over with the olive oil. Season generously with salt and pepper and roast in the oven for 25–30 minutes until the meat has taken on some colour and is already smelling delicious.

Remove the tray from the oven. Arrange the potatoes and garlic bulb halves around the mutton, turning the potatoes through the fat once or twice as you go. Season the potatoes and garlic with a little salt then, if using, tuck the hay around everything like you're a bird making a nest for your eggs. Cover the tray with a sheet of baking parchment followed by a sheet of foil. Crimp it up round the edges of the tray so it keeps the steam in. Reduce the oven temperature to 160°C/325°F/gas mark 3 and return the mutton to the middle of the oven and cook for a further 1½ hours.

While the mutton is cooking, make the green herb sauce. Place the parsley and mint on a board and use a nice sharp knife to chop it all up. Add the capers, mustard and grated garlic and carry on chopping until it's all fairly fine. Spoon into a bowl and add the vinegar and olive oil and season with salt and pepper to taste. It should have a loose-ish consistency, a bit like a dressing, so add a splash more oil or a tiny dash of water if it's a bit thick.

Remove the roasting tray from the oven, uncover and check the mutton is cooked to your liking, using a digital temperature probe if you have one. Check the potatoes are cooked too, if they're not quite there yet, return them to the oven to finish off. Either way, leave the meat to rest for 20–25 minutes.

To serve, carefully lift the mutton from the tray to a wooden board or a platter, give everyone a potato to split and butter, carve some nice slices of mutton for everyone and share out the roasted garlic and green herb sauce.

# Why Real Fat Is Back

———

Fat has a bad rap, and undeservedly so. From the 1970s, the advice for avoiding heart disease and other chronic health problems was to aim for a low-fat diet by eschewing red meat and butter and turning to lean meats and margarine instead. Low-fat and fat-free processed foods proliferated in one of the first examples of food manufacturers capitalizing on arguably oversimplified dietary advice, and images of sprightly, bright-eyed folk were used to advertize fat-free yogurts, spreads and margarines. An equally oversimplified direct correlation between body fat and the fat in our food has contributed to the demonization of this vital macronutrient too. However, humans are products of nature – and nature is far more complicated than that.

Fat is a crucial part of our diet as it has a pivotal role in protecting our organs, producing hormones, in cell growth and nutrient uptake, alongside many other biological processes. Our brains are a staggering 60% fat. From a strategic survival perspective, it is brilliant stuff, allowing the body to store energy for times when food is hard to come by, which was (evolutionarily speaking) quite often. Before we mastered the art of farming, food supply was unpredictable, so having a store of energy-dense material to power our bodies and brains is in no small part why humans are so successful as a species.

The most important thing to understand is that rather than how much fat we consume, it is the type of fat we need to put under a bit of scrutiny. While we don't advocate filling your metaphorical boots with lard, our view is that the most natural fat, that which our bodies have evolved to eat, is probably the best way to go for our health. There is also a strong environmental

argument too, once you look under the bonnet of how supposedly healthier vegetable oils are produced (clue: there ain't a vegetable in sight).

The starter ingredient of most margarines, vegetable spreads and vegetable cooking fats is oil from some kind of plant crop, such as rapeseed, sunflower, soybean or maize (or usually a blend of these). The majority of these will be sourced from vast monocultures, in one-size-fits-all farming systems designed to take from the soil, and feed global commodity trading, rather than the local community, its wildlife or natural landscape. While much of the oil can be extracted by milling or pressing the whole seed, a volatile solvent, usually hexane, is required to reach full extraction efficiency. The oils produced don't have a very good shelf life and are liquid at room temperature, so if you are after a solid, spreadable fat for sandwiches and baking, the oil must go through another industrial process to change its physical state and increase its stability. This chemical altering is called hydrogenation, whereby the fat molecule structure is rebuilt to make it more stable. The product may then go through deodorizing, while emulsifiers and colourants are also added depending on the desired qualities. In short, for all the glowing people you see prancing through fields in their ad campaigns, vegetable oils and spreads are some way off being a natural source of fat.

Before vegetable oils came on the scene, most people cooked with dairy and animal fats. It made sense; until industrialized butchery systems and supermarkets came along and created different industrial streams for parts of the carcass, animal fats in the form of tallow, suet, lard and butter were the only option for most British families. They were readily available

at the local butchers and formed part of the regular shop. By rendering the fats – slowly heating them on the hob – any water could be removed, giving them a decent shelf life. Without water, bacteria is unable to thrive, so even before the advent of refrigeration, a jar of tallow (rendered beef fat), or lard (rendered pork fat) could last a couple of months in a dark, cool corner of the farmhouse pantry. It is arguably a form of processing, but natural fats from grass-fed livestock involve far fewer chemical processes, agrochemicals, air freighting and anonymous food chains.

There's another layer to this story; fat is flavour. When an ultra-processed food is made low fat, more often than not a lot of the flavour disappears with it. The fats are replaced with sugar or starch to bring back some level of palatability, often a by-product of some other food process. The industrial food system needs to be viewed as a sort of sleight-of-hand shuffle, where by-products are combined and transformed with chemistry, additives and a dash of high-marketing-spend magic into ham slices with a pig's face or bear-shaped cakes.

Yet natural animal fats are your friend, when used judiciously. Typically they have a high smoke point, so you can fry and sear away, and better still they can impart beautiful flavour to your dishes. Less and better meat is part of our philosophy at Pipers Farm, and this applies to fat too. Because fat from slowly reared livestock has had more time to build up naturally, it really is loaded with flavour, so it goes further. Cooking vegetable dishes in animal fat is a brilliant way of reducing your overall meat intake without losing out on enjoyment. Alongside this is the natural body that animal fat imparts, that rich, silky mouthfeel that is so hard to emulate with anything else.

As for that animal-fat-dodging advice from the 70s and beyond, it turns out that a lot of it is being re-examined as the dark side of vegetable oils comes to light, and the benefits of animal fats are uncovered and championed. Fat from grass-fed animals have omega-3 and 6 oils that are essential for our health, as our bodies can't produce them alongside fat-soluble vitamins A, D, E and K that are in a form readily absorbed by the body. And they are simply delicious, they ensure every part of the animal is prized and respected, and on balance they are probably a lot kinder to people and planet than margarine and its oily friends.

*Natural animal fats
are your friend, when
used judiciously.*

## A QUICK GUIDE TO COOKING FATS

**Tallow** – Made from the fat from cows, this is also known as beef dripping, because of the way it used to be collected in a bowl below a slowly roasting piece of meat. Completely delicious, it was regularly spread on bread as a simple farmworker lunch and makes the finest Yorkshire puddings on the planet. Naturally firm at room temperature.

**Suet** – This is the hard fat from around the kidneys of cattle and sheep. It has a drier, more crumbly texture compared to the semi-solid nature of tallow or lard, and imparts an extraordinary richness of taste and texture to cooking. A wonderful traditional ingredient used in many old English favourites, most commonly Christmas puddings, hot water crust pastry and puds like spotted dick. Its high smoke point makes it perfect for frying and pastry making.

**Lard** – Rendered fat from pigs. This was what people used when they needed to make pastry; when dinner needed frying; and even as a quick breakfast, eaten smeared on a piece of bread. So much has changed in our recent history that this versatile product fell out of fashion. Softer and silkier than tallow, it brings a porky note to whatever you are cooking. Some industrially produced lard (usually from intensive pig farming) goes through hydrogenation to make it a solid block.

**Ghee** – A high smoke point version of butter. Butter will burn when used for frying and general cooking, as it has a relatively low smoke point due to the presence of milk solids. By slowly heating butter, these solids can be separated out, creating a versatile cooking oil with all the flavour, nutrients and qualities of beautiful butter.

## How to Confit Duck

This classic dish from south-west France was designed to sustain locals during the cold winter months. Locally reared birds would be slaughtered at the end of summer and then salted, cooked and stored in fat to preserve them throughout the winter.

**SERVES 6**

6 free-range duck legs
500g (1lb 2oz) free-range goose
 or duck fat, or enough
 to totally submerge
 the duck legs
3 bay leaves

*For the cure*
½ teaspoon cumin seeds,
 lightly toasted
12 coriander seeds,
 lightly toasted
½ teaspoon fennel seeds,
 lightly toasted
3 juniper berries
50g (1¾oz) pure flaky sea salt
1 small bunch of thyme,
 leaves picked
1 garlic clove
1 teaspoon black peppercorns

Gently crush all the cure ingredients using a pestle and mortar.

Place the duck legs into a tray and rub with the cure. Place the tray in the fridge and leave the duck legs to cure for 24 hours, turning them over a couple of times as they marinate.

Preheat the oven to 150°C/300°F/gas mark 2. Carefully pat the duck legs dry (don't wash off the marinade as the salt extracts the water from the cells, which will be reinflated with fat as the duck cooks).

Place the duck legs in a casserole dish and cover generously with fat, making sure the legs are completely submerged. Add the bay leaves and cook for about 2½ hours.

Store the cooked duck in a pudding bowl or Kilner jar, covered with the fat, in the fridge – as long as it stays covered with fat it will last for weeks. To cook the duck, heat an ovenproof pan on the hob until it is hot. Add the duck legs, skin-side down, and cook for 4 minutes until crisp, then cook in the oven at 180°C/350°F/gas mark 4 for a further 20 minutes. Serve with a green salad and crusty bread.

A classic French peasant-style dish, this recipe has been handed down through the generations from farmhouse table to farmhouse table. It is the perfect bowl of food to savour after a hard day's work out in the field.

# Confit Duck Cassoulet

## — SERVES 4 —

4 banana shallots
4 garlic cloves
500g (1lb 2oz) bacon lardons
1 pack free-range confit
   duck legs (see page 63)
2 x 400g (14oz) cans
   cannellini beans, drained
500ml (18fl oz) chicken stock
   (see page 21)
1 small bunch of oregano,
   chopped
100g (3½oz) breadcrumbs
a drizzle of extra virgin olive oil
1 small bunch of flat-leaf
   parsley, freshly chopped
pure sea salt and freshly
   ground black pepper

Preheat the oven to 160°C/325°F/gas mark 3.

In a casserole dish, add a drizzle of oil and fry the shallots, garlic and lardons together for 10 minutes until nicely softened and caramelized.

Prepare the confit duck legs by slicing through the joint in the middle of the leg to produce 2 nice pieces per leg. Add the duck to the pan along with the cannellini beans, stock, oregano, a pinch of salt and a few cracks of black pepper. Cook for 1½ hours until the beans have absorbed some of the stock and the mixture has thickened.

Remove the dish from the oven, scatter with the breadcrumbs and drizzle over some olive oil. Increase the oven temperature to 200°C/400°F/gas mark 6 and return the dish to the oven for a further 5–10 minutes to crisp up.

Scatter with the flat-leaf parsley and serve.

This simple dish could equally be served up at a French roadside restaurant, as well as around the farmhouse kitchen table here in Devon. It celebrates simple home-grown ingredients of free-range duck, 'just forked' potatoes and the freshest eggs – a selection of enterprises that many mixed family farms or smallholdings would have naturally have had in their yard.

# Duck Breast, Duck Fat Chips & Roast Garlic Aioli

## — SERVES 2 —

1kg (2lb 4oz) white potatoes, peeled and cut into thinnish wedges
50g (1¾oz) duck, goose or pork fat, plus extra for frying
1 small bunch of thyme
2 sprigs of rosemary
2 bay leaves
1 bulb of garlic
2 free-range duck breasts
pure sea salt and freshly ground black pepper

*For the roast garlic aioli*
2 very fresh free-range and/ or organic egg yolks
2 pinches of pure sea salt
1–2 sprigs of thyme, leaves picked and finely chopped
2 small, salted anchovy fillets, finely chopped (optional)
1 heaped teaspoon Dijon mustard
1 tablespoon cider vinegar or lemon juice
200ml (7fl oz) sunflower oil
150ml (5fl oz) extra virgin olive oil, plus extra for drizzling

*For the simple salad*
1 large or 2 small heads of chicory
1 large orange
2 tablespoons olive oil

Preheat the oven to 200°C/400°F/gas mark 6.

Place the potato wedges in a large pan, cover with salted water and bring to the boil over a high heat. Cook, uncovered, for 3–4 minutes. Drain and leave to steam off.

Meanwhile, spoon the fat over a roasting tray and pop it in the oven to heat up. When the fat is hot, carefully tip the potatoes on to the tray. Scatter over half the thyme, rosemary sprigs and bay leaves. Cut the first 1–2cm (½–¾in) from the top of the garlic bulb, which should expose the tips of each clove. Wrap the bulb in foil and pop it in the tray with the potatoes. Return the tray to the oven and cook for 35–45 minutes.

While this is happening, set a heavy cast-iron pan over a medium heat and add a dash more duck fat. Season the duck breasts all over with salt and pepper and lay them skin-side down in the pan. Cook gently for 10–12 minutes, then turn the duck breasts over and add the remaining herbs. Cook the duck for a further 4–5 minutes, then remove the pan from the heat, lift the duck out of the pan to a board, cover and leave it to rest somewhere warm.

Remove the garlic from the oven, carefully unwrap it and squeeze out the soft, sweet flesh into the bowl of a food processor. Add the egg yolks, salt, thyme, anchovy fillets (if using), Dijon mustard and cider vinegar. Whizz for 30–40 seconds. Combine the oils in a jug. With the motor running, start to add the oils to the food processor in a thin trickle. When the oil mixture starts to emulsify with the yolks and garlic, you can add it a little faster. If things have gone to plan, you will have a thick, glossy, garlicky mayonnaise. Cover and set aside.

Divide the chicory leaves and place them in a bowl. Finely grate over the orange zest and squeeze over the juice. Trickle over the olive oil and season with salt and pepper. Toss the leaves through the dressing.

To serve, thickly slice the duck and divide between 2 plates. Pile on the chips and serve with the aioli and the dressed salad.

It is now more common for the farm to be covered in a glittering coating of frost during the month of March than it is in December. Biting winds sweep across the countryside, these short dark days can often feel rather bleak, especially when each farm chore feels far more difficult than during the lazy, hazy days of summer. Forced rhubarb provides a much-needed burst of colour, a balm to the shades of grey, and makes a perfect ingredient to cheer during winter days. Early forced rhubarb is grown in the dark, in warm sheds from the end of winter and into the beginning of spring. The season is relatively short and so it is vital to make the most of these versatile pink spears while they are in season. This lovely light dish provides us with hope that warmer spring days are just around the corner.

# Black Pudding with Rhubarb & Chicory

## — SERVES 2 AS A STARTER —

2 tablespoons cider vinegar
2 tablespoons caster sugar
1 tablespoon water
4 small sticks of rhubarb,
  sliced into 1cm (½in) pieces
1 head of chicory
olive oil
2 thick slices of good-quality
  black pudding

*For the vinaigrette*
1 tablespoon Dijon mustard
1 teaspoon cider vinegar
1 teaspoon caster sugar
2 tablespoons extra virgin
  olive oil
1 small bunch of dill,
  finely chopped
pure sea salt and freshly
  ground black pepper

Put the cider vinegar, sugar and water in a small pan and bring to the boil. Add the sliced rhubarb and gently cook for 2–3 minutes in the cider vinegar mixture, so the rhubarb softens but doesn't fall apart. Set aside to cool.

Prepare the vinaigrette for the chicory. Whisk together the mustard, cider vinegar and sugar. Slowly drizzle in the olive oil, whisking constantly to form a thick, glossy dressing. Stir through the chopped dill. Divide the chicory leaves and dress thoroughly.

Heat a small, heavy-based frying pan over a medium heat, add a drizzle of oil and fry the pieces of black pudding for 5 minutes until dark and crispy.

Serve the three elements alongside one another on small plates.

Liver is one of the few foods we truly believe is worthy of the title 'superfood'. One of the most nutritionally dense foods on the planet, it is not only rich in protein but packed full of essential vitamins and minerals. This take on the classic liver and mash showcases the depth of flavour ox liver carries and why liver was once a popular and treasured food source. The wild garlic mash is a lovely way to celebrate the near arrival of spring and provides brightness against the spectacular richness of ox liver.

# Ox Liver & Onions with Wild Garlic Mash

— SERVES 4 —

*For the wild garlic mash*
500g (1lb 2oz) large white
   potatoes, peeled and chopped
100ml (3½fl oz) single cream
a pinch of pure sea salt
a pinch of freshly ground
   black pepper
75g (2¾oz) grass-fed butter
a large handful of wild garlic
   leaves, finely chopped,
   plus extra small leaves to
   serve (optional; you can use
   roughly chopped flat-leaf
   parsley or finely chopped
   spring onions instead)

*For the ox liver and onions*
olive oil
2 onions, finely sliced
2 garlic cloves, finely chopped
250ml (9fl oz) white wine
200ml (7fl oz) beef stock
   (see page 22)
500g (1lb 2oz) ox liver
2 tablespoons stoneground
   unbleached white flour
a knob of grass-fed butter,
   for frying
1 teaspoon freshly
   chopped thyme
1 teaspoon freshly
   chopped sage
pure sea salt and freshly
   ground black pepper

Put the potatoes in a large saucepan, cover with salted water and bring to the boil. Simmer the potatoes for about 20 minutes until tender and then drain. Leave the potatoes to steam in a colander for a few minutes to dry out.

In a small saucepan, heat the cream until boiling. Take the potatoes out of the colander and place them back into the large saucepan. Pour over the warm cream. Season the potatoes with a generous pinch of salt and pepper. Mash the potatoes together with the cream until smooth, then stir in the butter in small chunks followed by the wild garlic. Cover the surface of the mash with a sheet of baking parchment while you prepare the liver and onions.

Heat a drizzle of olive oil in a frying pan and fry the onions and garlic for 5 minutes until they have started to soften. Increase the heat and add the white wine to the frying pan and reduce the liquid until it has all but disappeared. When the wine has reduced, add the stock and herbs and gently simmer for about 10 minutes until the onion mixture is thick, saucy and rich.

Meanwhile, heat a second large frying pan over a medium–high heat. Dust the slices of liver with the flour and season thoroughly with salt and pepper. Add the butter to the pan and, when it is smoking hot, add the slices of liver along with the herbs, avoiding crowding the pan (it may be necessary to do this in batches).

Fry the liver aggressively on both sides for 1 minute. Once the liver has a good amount of colour, transfer to the pan alongside the onions.

Stir the onions and liver together so the liver is coated with the thick stock-based sauce.

Warm through the mash and dish up alongside the liver and onions, dressing the plate with a few small wild garlic leaves if you have them.

Good ol'-fashioned chicken and dumplings are an absolute winner for anyone's kitchen table. Here, melt-in-the-mouth chicken is coupled with a deliciously creamy broth and gloriously savoury dumplings. This dish is perfect all year round due to the majority of its ingredients being storecupboard staples. A top tip when cooking the dumplings – if you're unsure whether the dumplings are ready or not, stick a toothpick or skewer into a dumpling after the specified cooking time. If it comes out clean, then the dumplings are ready to be dished up.

# Chicken Stew with Tarragon Dumplings

— SERVES 3 —

olive oil
1 onion, diced
2 garlic cloves, sliced
2 tablespoons stoneground unbleached white flour
6 chicken thighs
1 litre (1¾ pints) chicken stock (see page 21)
1 sprig of rosemary
200ml (7fl oz) double cream
2 tablespoons Dijon mustard
pure sea salt and freshly ground black pepper
a handful of freshly chopped chives, to garnish

*For the dumplings*
150g (5½oz) stoneground unbleached white flour
75g (2¾oz) grass-fed beef suet
1 small bunch of tarragon, freshly chopped

In a deep, heavy-based, ovenproof pan, add a drizzle of olive oil, the onion, garlic and 2 tablespoons of flour and gently fry until soft. Once softened, add the chicken thighs, chicken stock and rosemary. Stir and then leave to simmer over a low heat for 1½ hours.

After 1½ hours the chicken should be tender to touch and will come off the bone extremely easily. Remove from the pan and pick the chicken meat from the bones. Add the meat back into the broth and then discard the bones.

Bring to a simmer, then gradually stir in the double cream and mustard and leave on low while you make the dumplings.

To make the dumplings, combine the flour and suet with the tarragon and a good pinch of salt. Divide into 9 equal-sized balls.

Preheat oven to 180°C/350°F/gas mark 4.

When the stew has slightly thickened, add the dumplings to the surface. Place a lid on the pan and cook in the oven for 15 minutes, then remove the lid and return to the oven for a further 15 minutes to allow the dumplings to take on some colour. Garnish with the chives and serve with a crisp green salad.

# April

The return of the swallows to the barns is a treasured milestone of the farming year. The swifts and house martins follow close behind, bringing with them their raucous calls, sweeping flights, mid-air feeding and devoted nest building.

In the kitchen we have hit the hungry gap, where the British roots and greens are in short supply before the new season kicks in. Traditionally, gathering nettle tops and verdant wild garlic from the shady lanes and copses sees us through, and we look forward to the abundance to come in the kitchen garden as we plant out seedlings.

Often when we think of cockerels we think of scrawny, worn-out birds, not so in this case! Our cockerels have been running around idyllic pastures for over 125 days, and all this foraging and free-ranging builds up seriously strong carcasses, ligaments and muscles – which rewards you with so much flavour. Little fuss is needed to make this bird sing. Take a slab of smoky, fat-rich streaky bacon, a few new season potatoes and carrots, some vibrant parsley and some seriously hot mustard – as hot as you can stand it – and you have a dish that is humble yet so utterly delicious.

# Pot-roast Cockerel with Smoked Bacon, Carrots, Potatoes & Parsley

— SERVES 6 —

1 free-range cockerel
   or chicken
1 tablespoon olive oil
500g (1lb 2oz) piece
   of smoked bacon
6–8 large carrots,
   scrubbed or peeled
6 small onions
1 bulb of garlic
a few bay leaves
800g (1lb 12 oz) white
   potatoes, peeled and
   cut into bite-sized chunks
1 small bunch of parsley,
   leaves freshly chopped
pure sea salt and freshly
   ground black pepper
Green Herb Sauce
   (see page 56), to serve

Preheat the oven to 220°C/425°F/gas mark 7.

Rub the bird with oil and season it all over with salt and pepper. Place the bird and the bacon in your largest lidded casserole dish. Place the casserole in the oven, without a lid at this point, and roast the bird and bacon for 25–30 minutes. You want them to take on a little colour, but not brown too much.

Remove the dish from the oven and add the carrots, onions, garlic and bay leaves pour over enough water to cover the chicken and bacon. Reduce the oven temperature to 180°C/350°F/gas mark 4. Place a lid on the dish and return to the oven for 2 hours.

Lift the lid and add the potatoes to the casserole dish. It may be a bit of a jostle for space, but they should fit. Replace the lid and return the pan to the oven for a further 30–40 minutes or until the potatoes are cooked.

Remove the casserole dish from the oven. Generously sprinkle the parsley over the chicken and bacon, season the broth with plenty of salt and pepper and bring the dish to the table to rest.

To serve, lift the cockerel out of the casserole on to a large platter. Set the bacon down alongside it and spoon the vegetables around the sides. Carve the cockerel and bacon and divide between bowls, give everybody some vegetables and ladle over some broth. Serve with good bread, mustard and green herb sauce.

# Abbatoirs – the Keystone of Local Food Systems

By rearing livestock on home-grown grass and feed, small-scale family farmers are not reliant on the complex global supply chains that are integral to how industrialized farming systems operate. It's a way of producing meat that requires little more than grass, sunshine and a respectful relationship with nature. This makes them more fleet of foot and resilient compared to the industrial-scale big boys whose farming is focused on spreadsheets, carbon-hungry artificial fertilizer and flown-in feed.

Yet a beautifully reared animal from a nearby farm is no good to anyone until it is slaughtered. For centuries this country had a network of small-scale abattoirs, where local farms could bring their livestock for a respectful, humane slaughter, with minimal travel and stress. This is especially important for rare breeds that need particularly skilled management. Yet one-size-fits-all legislation, which treats these small operations the same as enormous industrial slaughterhouses that supply the supermarkets, alongside rising costs and the collapse in price of hides and skins, has led to a third of small abattoirs closing in the past ten years alone.

These micro-abattoirs are the keystone of resilient local food systems, and have a huge role in UK food security. Without them, livestock will have to travel long distances before slaughter, increasing stress levels and impacting animal welfare and meat quality significantly. Meanwhile, highly geared industrial slaughterhouses have only one focus: speed. The quicker they process, the more money they make. They have no interest in small numbers, which means if we lose access to low-throughput, local abattoirs there will be nowhere for smallholders to take their livestock to kill. This would see a dramatic shift in our countryside and the communities who live within it. In one fell swoop, it could wipe out the local food chain.

Utilizing a skilled local abattoir means that we can close the loop in true artisan meat. Large-scale slaughterhouses use huge amounts of water in the process, resulting in poorer-quality wet meat that is unsuitable to be hung. It is also not always possible to get the offal back from them either, which means not only are we wasting a key source of nutrition but we could be losing a part of our culture – food that has been a staple on the table for hundreds of years.

As farming subsidies are phased out, farmers will need to champion what is special about their livestock all the more, including how the animals are reared, so that meat produced under greater care gets the price it deserves. Selling these animals into anonymized meat markets where they become a commodity, and no longer a rare breed carcass of remarkable meat, is a travesty. Without local abattoirs to serve local farmers, they are also unable to market their own meat direct, and that means fewer family farmers, fewer rural jobs and the loss of rare, native breeds.

As farmers, we are part of nature, a complex system that requires an unwavering respect for all natural life. Death too is part of nature, and disconnecting ourselves from this only opens the door to abuse. If we do not properly scrutinize every part of the rearing and processing of meat, we are opening ourselves up to increasing domination of factory farming and globalized food production.

Local abattoirs offer the truly artisan craft of unrushed, ethical and humane slaughter to small-scale farmers, and they must be protected. Giving them the support they need to go on serving our local food system and our rural economy is crucial for a sustainable, robust food system. After all, with no slaughter, there's no meat.

# How to Butcher a Bird

———

**What you'll need:**

A robust knife with a firm and sharp blade

A sturdy wooden chopping board (pop a damp towel underneath to keep it in place)

**How to joint a bird**

*To remove the wings:* Place the whole chicken, breast up, on your chopping board. Pull the wing out straight, away from the bird. With your knife, with one firm downward cut, as close to the body as possible, chop the wing away from the bird.

*To remove the legs:* Pull the leg away from the body and slice through the skin between the breast and the thigh. Then push the leg downwards until the ball of the thigh bone tears away from the socket. Cut through all attaching sinews and the leg should come away easily.

Divide the legs into drumstick and thigh. Feel with your fingers the joint in the leg, slice cleanly through this join and you will end up with a portion of thigh and drumstick.

*To remove the breast:* Feel the carcass bone down the centre of the breast. Turn your knife to a slight angle and make a long cut against the bone, you should now be able to see how close you are to the carcass. Using your fingers you will be able to gently pull the breast away from the carcass – keeping as little meat on the carcass as possible. With your knife, carefully cut away the bottom of the breast following all the way around the bird, past the wishbone, until the breast has come free.

You can also separate the fillet from the breast to create another meal. This will gently tear away from the breast.

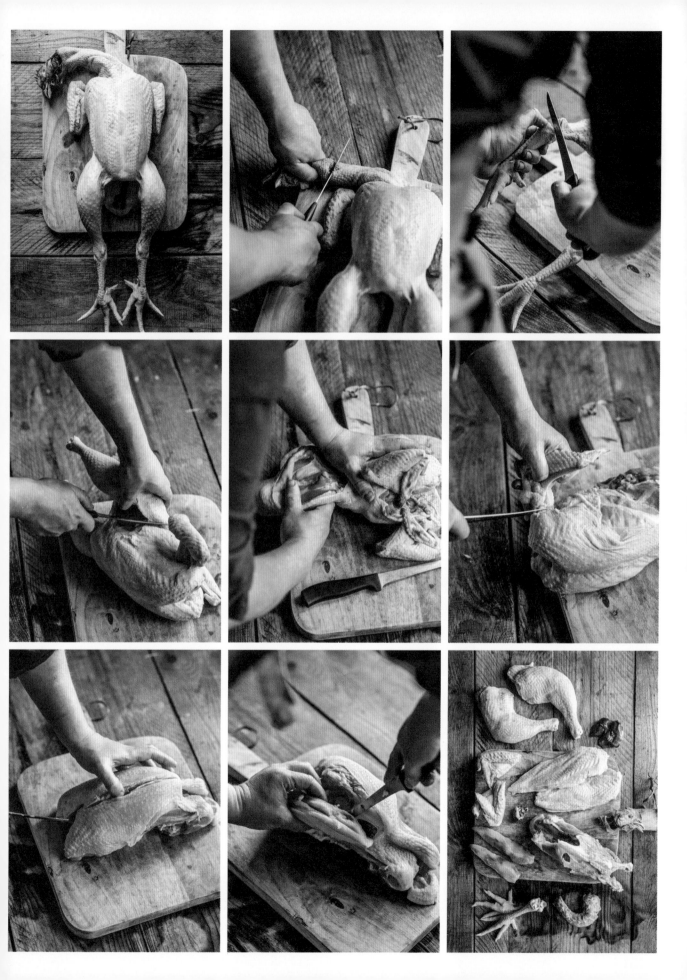

Traditionally coq au vin would have been made using an old cockerel or an egg-laying hen that had come to the end of its breeding life. The recipe was designed as a resourceful way to use up the spent birds, cooking them long and slow (as they would have been very tough), with plenty of wine – which was probably made from grapes grown near the chickens – and few other ingredients. It originated as peasant food that would have been fed to farmworkers at low cost. It is the perfect recipe to celebrate the life of our free-ranging birds, which spend their days running around outside, leading a life well lived – like their French counterparts from a bygone age.

# Coq au Vin

## — SERVES 4 —

olive oil
2 chicken thighs on the bone
2 chicken drumsticks
1 chicken neck
200g (7oz) bacon lardons
4 banana shallots, halved
300g (10½oz) chestnut
    mushrooms, quartered
750ml (1¼ pints) red wine,
    plus extra (if necessary)
4 bay leaves
4 sprigs of thyme
4 garlic cloves, bashed
500ml (18fl oz) chicken
    stock (see page 21)
1 small bunch of flat-leaf
    parsley, freshly chopped
pure sea salt and freshly
    ground black pepper

Preheat the oven to 180°C/350°F/gas mark 4.

Generously season the chicken pieces with olive oil, salt and pepper.

Begin by heating a wide, heavy-based frying pan. Add a splash of olive oil and fry the lardons until the fat begins to render and the lardons become crispy and golden. Remove the lardons from the pan and set to one side. Using the same pan, brown the chicken thighs, drumsticks and neck in the bacon fat. Remove the chicken from the pan and set to one side. Fry off the shallots and mushrooms until they take on some colour and just begin to soften.

Take a large, lidded casserole dish and add the wine along with the bay leaves, thyme and garlic. Place over a low heat and simmer gently, uncovered, until the liquid has reduced by half.

To the casserole dish, add the chicken pieces, lardons, vegetables and chicken stock. Place the lid on, transfer to the oven and gently cook for 1½ hours. You will need to check the liquid from time to time and top up with more red wine if it is looking dry.

Remove from the oven and leave to stand for 10 minutes. Scatter with the flat-leaf parsley and serve with mash and seasonal greens.

As good on a chilly April day, as it is on a gloriously sunny one. That's the beauty of Scandinavian inspired cookery, many dishes work equally well in the depths of winter as they do on lighter brighter days, making them a perfect choice for changeable April. This recipe is a real family favourite, a classic we turn to time and time again.

# Pork Schnitzel with Dill Potato Salad & Quick Pickled Cucumbers

— SERVES 4 —

*For the pickled cucumbers*
½ cucumber, halved, deseeded and thinly sliced
60g (2¼oz) caster sugar
100ml (3½fl oz) cider vinegar
3 cloves
1 teaspoon coriander seeds

*For the potato salad*
2 free-range and/or organic eggs, hard-boiled and cooled
2 teaspoons Dijon mustard
100ml (3½fl oz) soured cream
800g (1lb 12oz) salad potatoes, cooked and cooled
4 spring onions, finely sliced
2 tablespoons freshly chopped dill, plus extra to garnish

*For the schnitzel*
60g (2¼oz) stoneground unbleached white flour
1 free-range and/or organic egg
100g (3½oz) panko breadcrumbs
4 native breed pork escalopes
2 tablespoons olive oil
a generous knob of grass-fed butter
pure sea salt and freshly ground black pepper

Place the cucumber in a bowl and lightly season with salt. Put the sugar, vinegar, cloves and coriander seeds into a small saucepan and heat gently until the sugar has dissolved. Remove from the heat and leave to cool. Pour the cooled liquid over the cucumbers and leave for at least 15 minutes, the longer the better, to allow the pickle to penetrate. You can do this well in advance if you like.

Peel the boiled eggs and coarsely chop them. Add them to a mixing bowl with the mustard and soured cream. Roughly chop the potatoes and throw them in too, along with the spring onions and dill. Season with salt and pepper and mix well. Garnish with a little extra dill.

Tip the flour into a shallow bowl. Crack the egg into a second bowl and beat it thoroughly with a dash of water. Tip the breadcrumbs into a third bowl and mix well. Season the escalopes generously with salt and pepper on both sides. One at a time, turn each escalope in the flour until evenly coated, shaking away the excess. Dip and drag it through the egg so that it is coated. Then throw it into the breadcrumbs, turning and pressing until completely coated. Repeat with all the escalopes. Keep to one side.

Put a large frying pan over a medium heat. Add the oil and butter. Once the butter has melted and begun to foam, add the schnitzels to the pan and fry for 2–3 minutes per side until golden brown and cooked through.

Serve them immediately with the potato salad and pickled cucumbers on the side.

As we meander down Devon country lanes there are a scattering of 'rustic' handmade signs adorning farm gates and showcasing to the passer-by what is available down a bumpy track. There is no sign that gets us more excited to pull over and hop out of the car than reading 'new season asparagus available', usually scrawled on a bit of old timber. Bunches of green spears are neatly gathered together and secured with an elastic band, sitting alongside a rusty old honesty box. Or sometimes it is through a farm's kitchen window that a few coins are passed in exchange for a bouquet of veg.

The asparagus season is fleeting – just six weeks or so – and that's how we like it, enthusiastically enjoying this seasonal star while it's available, then bidding farewell when the season's over. After all, doesn't it taste better when it's long awaited?

# Bacon, Asparagus & Goat's Cheese Galette
## — SERVES 4 —

olive oil
250g (9oz) bacon lardons
1 leek, washed and sliced
1 free-range and/or organic egg
100g (3½oz) crème fraîche
1 small bunch of asparagus,
   woody ends removed
150g (5½oz) fresh goat's
   cheese or curd
a handful of dill, fronds picked
zest of 1 lemon
pure sea salt and freshly
   ground black pepper

*For the pastry*
180g (6oz) unsalted
   grass-fed butter, chilled
360g (12½oz) stoneground
   unbleached white flour,
   plus extra for dusting
3–4 tablespoons cold water
1 free-range and/or organic
   egg, beaten

For the pastry, dice the butter and combine with the flour and a pinch of salt in a bowl. Add the water and mix together to form a tight dough.

Dust your work surface with flour and roll out the dough to a thickness of about 2cm (¾in). Bring the ends of the pastry together so they overlap. Turn the dough by a quarter and roll out again. Repeat this process 3 more times. Wrap the pastry in clingfilm or baking parchment and chill in the fridge for 30 minutes.

Heat a heavy-based frying pan on the hob, then add a drizzle of oil followed by the bacon lardons. Cook until the bacon is golden and crisp and some of the fat from the lardons has rendered. Remove the lardons from the pan, retaining the fat. Add the leek and sweat down until soft and sweet but it hasn't taken on any colour.

Transfer the leek to a bowl and combine with the egg and crème fraîche. Stir to combine and season well.

Preheat the oven to 180°C/350°F/gas mark 4 and line a large baking tray with baking parchment.

Roll out the pastry to form a disc just slightly wider than the dimensions of the baking tray and place on the lined tray.

Top the pastry with the leek and crème fraîche mixture, followed by the asparagus and lardons. Roughly crimp the outsides of the pastry to form a border. Brush the pastry with the beaten egg. Bake for 25–30 minutes until the pastry is golden and crisp and the asparagus is nicely cooked.

Finish with dots of goat's cheese, the dill and lemon zest.

This is a wonderful recipe to show you how a little meat can go a long way. The protein-rich lentils play the starring role in this dish, with sausages taking on a supporting act. We have suggested that this recipe feeds four but you could easily stretch it to six if you allow fewer sausages per person. The salsa verde is simply non-negotiable here, the vibrant sharpness does wonders to cut through the richness of this dish. The whole thing freezes perfectly too.

# Sausages with Green Lentils & Salsa Verde

## — SERVES 4 —

300g (10½oz) green lentils
   (we like Hodmedod's)
olive oil
250g (9oz) bacon lardons
1 onion, finely diced
2 celery sticks, finely diced
2 carrots, peeled and
   finely diced
2 bay leaves
3 garlic cloves, finely chopped
6 natural plain pork sausages
a splash of cider vinegar
pure sea salt and freshly
   ground black pepper

*For the salsa verde*
1 small bunch of basil
1 small bunch of
   flat-leaf parsley
1 small bunch of mint
2 garlic cloves
1 tablespoon capers,
   rinsed
1 tablespoon cider vinegar,
   plus extra to taste
4 tablespoons olive oil
3–4 anchovy fillets

Rinse the lentils in cold running water and leave to soak for 30 minutes.

To make the salsa verde, chop all the ingredients by hand or use a blender or food processor. Finely chop the herbs, garlic and capers together, add the vinegar and olive oil, next add the anchovies along with a good pinch of salt and also some black pepper, blitz to combine. Check the seasoning, adding more salt and pepper, as necessary.

Heat a drizzle of olive oil in a large pan, add the lardons and cook for about 5 minutes until crispy and golden. To the pan, add the onion, celery, carrots and bay leaves and cook for 10 minutes over a medium–low heat until very, very soft but without much colour. Add the garlic and cook for a further 2 minutes.

Add the soaked and drained lentils and 1 teaspoon of salt and stir until the lentils are well coated with the oil and vegetables, then add enough cold water to cover the lentils by about 1cm (½in). Bring to the boil, then reduce the heat to a simmer and cook the lentils for about 30 minutes until tender, or to your liking. Keep an eye on the pan and top up with a little more boiling water if necessary.

With the lentils cooking, fry the sausages in a drizzle of oil over a medium–low heat for 8–10 minutes until cooked through and nicely bronzed. Remove from the heat.

Remove the lentils from the heat and add a splash of vinegar to taste, checking the seasoning, adding more salt and pepper if necessary.

Serve the lentils with the sausages and a big dollop of salsa verde.

# May

The grass has now really found its feet, and we can turn out
the cattle. Too soon and their feet would poach the soil, destroying
its complex structure and the root systems of the dormant pasture.
Few could not take delight in seeing a 1,000kg (2,200lb) cow kick
up his heels on a moorland hill.

Spring is finding its way into the kitchen too, as we embrace
lighter dishes that sing of the season. Poultry, asparagus and
the first early herbs find their way to the table, bringing the
renewal we've been waiting for.

This little-known cut hails from South America where it is usually enjoyed cooked over fire on an asado. Cut from the rump, this stunning piece of meat is a combination of the most wonderful buttery fat which caramelizes beautifully over fire with tender, rich, beefy meat that releases so much flavour with each bite. Sweet, smoky and creamy, the partnership of new season carrots, smoky paprika and luscious beans are wonderful bedfellows to this indulgent cut.

# Fire-cooked Picanha with Roast Carrots, Smashed White Beans, Red Onions, Smoked Paprika, Nuts & Seeds

— SERVES 4 —

1 large or 2 smaller picanha steaks, weighing about 800g–1kg (1lb 12oz–2lb 4oz) in total
4–5 sprigs of thyme
pure sea salt and freshly ground black pepper

*For the carrots*
750g–1kg (1lb 10oz–2lb 4oz) organic carrots, peeled, trimmed and halved from top to tail
3 small–medium red onions, cut into wedges
2 garlic cloves, thickly sliced
2 teaspoons coriander seeds, crushed
2 teaspoons cumin seeds, crushed
1 teaspoon chilli flakes
1 teaspoon smoked paprika
2 tablespoons pumpkin seeds
2 tablespoons sunflower seeds
2 tablespoons olive oil
3–4 sprigs of rosemary

*For the smashed beans*
3 tablespoons extra virgin olive oil
2 garlic cloves, grated
2 x 400g (14oz) cans white beans, such as cannellini or butter beans, drained
zest and juice of 1 lemon
2 sprigs of rosemary
2 tablespoons tahini
2–3 tablespoons water

Preheat the oven to 200°C/400°F/gas mark 6.

Take your largest roasting tray and add the carrots, red onions, garlic, crushed coriander and cumin seeds, chilli flakes, paprika, pumpkin and sunflower seeds, olive oil, rosemary and plenty of salt and pepper. Turn the carrots and onions through the spices and oil. Place the tray in the oven and roast for 45 minutes–1 hour, stirring regularly, until all the carrots are tender (big ones might take as long as 1 hour).

Meanwhile, make the smashed beans. Heat 1 tablespoon of the olive oil in a medium frying pan over a medium–high heat, then add the garlic. Fry for 25–30 seconds until the garlic begins to soften, then add the white beans, lemon zest and rosemary. Stir to combine and cook for a further 1–2 minutes until the white beans are warmed through. Now, stir in the tahini, lemon juice and water. Cook for a further 1–2 minutes, then use a potato masher to break up some of the beans so they become thicker and creamier. Add a dash more water if you need to. Season to taste and set aside.

Fill the bottom of your barbecue with sustainable lumpwood charcoal and light. Allow the coals to heat until they form a grey coat, then add a few small logs to create a bit more smoke.

Season the steak(s) with lots of salt and pepper and sprinkle over the thyme. Lay the steaks and herbs on the grill, herbs down, and cook for 8–12 minutes on each side. If using a digital temperature probe, the internal temperature should be about 55°C (131°F) for just this side of medium-rare. Leave the steaks to rest for 5–8 minutes while you spoon out the beans over a large serving platter. Arrange the roast carrots and onions over the top and finish with some nice thick slices of steak.

# Anatomy of a Cowpat

At Pipers Farm, we prefer to travel with a cowpat. It starts with finding the right specimen, which must be at the correct stage of maturity – not so sloppy that it can't be transported, nor so desiccated that the more substantial wildlife has left the building. One with a decent crust but still moist within is the ticket. 'Harvesting' is a delicate operation that requires a shovel, a chopping board and commitment to the cause.

When we tell our farming story, we are direct about how our family history initially took a wrong turn in the 1970s and 80s, joining the march towards scale and intensification with a chicken farming enterprise. Ultimately we chose a different path through the founding of Pipers Farm and the cowpat that accompanies us at talks and events is our wingman in this storytelling. It comes with a cast of attention-grabbing characters, in the form of flora, fauna and just a little aroma.

As cattle are to an extent inefficient at digesting food, there is plenty of nutrition left in the cowpat once it hits the pasture. This, along with the fact that it is a warm and moist medium (cowpats are over 70% water), means each pat creates a mini-explosion of biodiversity. From microbes to nematodes, fungi to earthworms, grubs to beetles, flies, birds, bats and beyond, the trophic cascade each cowpat creates is Attenborough-worthy but it's the bugs that are the stars of the show. Insects are crucial for biodiversity and healthy ecosystems, and cowpats deserve plaudits for their role as bug nurseries. Given that a typical cow produces 7-10 cowpats a day, each of which ultimately supports around 1,000 developing insects, the basic 'cowpat maths' by one notable scientific study is such that each cow is powering the existence of 2.2 million insects a year. When coupled with the conservation services that carefully managed cattle can provide through grazing plant species that would otherwise out-compete rarer plants, a powerful picture of the biodiversity-boosting potential of cattle and their cowpats emerges. Ultimately the nutrients in the cowpat are released into the soil by the thrumming microbial activity, through incredibly complex biochemical pathways, plant-root interactions and mind-boggling fungal networks in the soil.

Yet modern farming techniques and world economics have skewed these processes. In industrial beef production where animals are mass treated, rather than given individual care, routine prophylactic use of wormers or antibiotics is common. This is the administration of medicine as a preventative measure to boost meat production. It has a significant impact on the gut biome of the cow and the life of the cowpat and beyond, with one scientific study finding 50% more insects in cowpats on organic farms, where routine wormer use is prohibited.

Intensively reared cattle, bred to grow fast on an unnatural diet of monoculture-fuelled feed may meet our need for ever-more meat, but it is clear that industrial beef is no friend to biodiversity when you consider what comes out of the other end. Acidic, dead and dangerously polluting, slurry (the liquid manure from indoor-kept cattle) can be a huge problem.

The Pipers Farm approach is simple, and it goes back to nature. Native breeds of cattle, which thrive on diverse pasture and convert grass into beautiful meat from nothing but sunshine. Small-scale mixed farms where herds can be rotated through fields in short, sharp bursts of mob grazing that stimulate growth and boost biodiversity without compacting the precious soil. No prophylactic use of wormers or antibiotics. Individual care of animals by families who know every inch of their farms. Reverence of cowpats is optional, but we find they are usually as obsessed with them as we are!

This recipe is a celebration of everything that is really great to eat at this time of year. Beautiful grass-fed beef that has been grazing on herb-rich pastures is carefully charred, rested and sliced alongside new season asparagus, vibrant broad beans (double podded, of course), fresh garden peas and a zingy herby dressing which lovingly brings the whole assortment together.

# Salad of Sirloin Steak, Asparagus, Peas, Broad Beans & Herbs

— SERVES 2 —

250g (9oz) broad beans
250g (9oz) peas
6–8 spears of asparagus
2 grass-fed sirloin steaks
olive oil
100g (3½oz) grass-fed butter,
    cut into 2 x 50g (1¾oz) pieces
3–4 tablespoons water
a small handful of fennel
    fronds (optional)
chive flowers (optional)
pure sea salt and freshly
    ground black pepper

*For the dressing*
1 small bunch of
    flat-leaf parsley
1 small bunch of mint
1 small bunch of dill
1 tablespoon capers
2 garlic cloves,
    finely chopped
juice of 1 lemon
olive oil

Pick the leaves from the stalks of the parsley, mint and dill and combine with the capers and garlic. Blend together in a food processor, adding lemon juice and olive oil to create a thick herby dressing, then season to taste.

Prepare the vegetables by podding the beans and peas if necessary and snapping off any tough ends of the asparagus.

Set a large, heavy-based frying pan over a high heat. Season the steaks with plenty of olive oil, salt and pepper. When the pan is hot, add the steaks and cook for 2 minutes on each side for rare, and for a further minute on each side for medium-rare. When the steaks have finished cooking, add 50g (1¾oz) of the butter to the pan and set aside to rest.

While the steaks are resting, cook the veg. Preheat a wide sauté pan on the stove, add the second piece of butter and the water and bring to the boil. Add the beans to the pan and cook for 1 minute before adding the asparagus and peas. Bubble away until the asparagus, peas and beans are tender and bright green.

Slice the sirloin steaks with a sharp knife and season the slices with a touch more salt and pepper. Scatter the vegetables on a wide platter alongside the slices of sirloin. Dress the salad with the herby dressing and finish with a scattering of fennel fronds and some chive flowers if you have them to hand.

This recipe is pure joy. A subtle celebration of a few delicious seasonal ingredients that work so harmoniously together. When it comes to making the tartare, there is nothing to be scared of, the most important tip we can provide is simply to use excellent-quality beef, the best you can find, from a fabulous farmer who has reared it in harmony with nature.

# Beef Tartare with Pickled Walnuts & Shallots

— SERVES 2 —

2 tablespoons cider vinegar
1 teaspoon caster sugar
1 small banana shallot
300g (10½oz) beef fillet
a small handful of flat-leaf
    parsley, finely chopped,
    plus extra to serve
1 pickled walnut,
    finely chopped
juice of ½ lemon
olive oil
2 walnuts, roughly chopped
pure sea salt

Combine the cider vinegar and sugar with a pinch of salt in a small bowl and stir until the sugar has dissolved. Finely slice the shallot into very thin slices. Place them in the vinegar mixture and leave for 15 minutes to soften and lightly pickle.

Trim the beef fillet to remove any sinew. Finely dice into 5mm (¼in) cubes. Place in a bowl and combine with the parsley, pickled walnut and lemon juice alongside a glug of olive oil and generous sprinkle of salt.

Serve on small plates, decorated with the pickled shallots, chopped walnuts and finely chopped flat-leaf parsley.

The earthy flavour of slow-grown hogget works so well with the smoky char from cooking over fire. Combine this with the freshness of ewe's curd, preserved lemon and new season asparagus and you have a perfect spring meal. Butterflying the lamb makes it so easy to cook and encourages more of the meat to take up that wonderful charred flavour you only get when cooking over fire.

# Butterflied Leg of Lamb, Ewe's Curd & Asparagus

— SERVES 8 —

2kg (4lb 8oz) butterflied
    leg of lamb
olive oil
1 preserved lemon
a handful of mint
200g (7oz) ewe's curd
    or feta cheese
2 bunches of asparagus,
    woody ends removed
1 bunch of radishes,
    thinly sliced
pure sea salt and freshly
    ground black pepper

Fill the bottom of your barbecue with sustainable lumpwood charcoal. Light the coals and allow them to heat up and develop a grey coat.

Season the lamb with a generous amount of salt and pepper and drizzle with olive oil. Place the lamb over the bed of hot embers and gently caramelize for about 10 minutes on each side, then move to one side of the grill where the temperature is cooler and gently cook through for about 30 minutes. If you are using a digital temperature probe, the temperature you are aiming for is 44°C (111°F) in the centre of the thickest part of the joint. Once cooked, remove the lamb from the grill, wrap in foil and leave to rest for 15 minutes.

Finely chop the preserved lemon and the mint. In a mixing bowl, combine the lemon, mint and ewe's curd, then season well with salt and pepper.

Lightly oil the asparagus and season with salt. Grill the asparagus for a maximum of 3 minutes – you still want a little crunch.

Slice the lamb leg and serve with the seasoned curd, grilled asparagus and thin slices of radish.

These koftas are built for the barbecue, especially when cooked over wood or coals as the smokiness makes the fat, spices and fresh herbs sing. The flatbreads couldn't be easier. They are perfect for beginners as they require no lengthy rising, shaping or baking. As long as you can knead dough and use a rolling pin you can't fail.

# Minty Lamb Koftas
# with Homemade Flatbreads
## — SERVES 8 —

*For the koftas*
1kg (2lb 4oz) grass-fed
    lamb mince
1 red onion, finely chopped
4 garlic cloves, finely chopped
1 tablespoon ground coriander
2 teaspoons ground cumin
1 teaspoon ground cinnamon
½ teaspoon chilli flakes,
    or to taste
3 tablespoons freshly
    chopped parsley
1 tablespoon freshly
    chopped mint
olive oil
pure sea salt and freshly
    ground black pepper
8 wooden barbecue skewers
    (soaked in water to stop
    them burning)

*For the flatbreads*
300g (10½oz) stoneground
    unbleached white flour,
    plus extra for dusting
1 tablespoon olive oil
½ teaspoon fine salt
180ml (6fl oz) warm water

*For the tahini yogurt*
150g (5½oz) yogurt
3 tablespoons tahini
juice of ½ lemon
½ teaspoon ground cumin
1 teaspoon freshly
    chopped mint

Put the lamb mince into a mixing bowl and add the onion, garlic, spices and chopped herbs. Season generously with salt and pepper. Get your hands into the bowl and thoroughly mix everything together. Shape the mixture into 8 fat sausages, making sure they are fairly compact. Take the skewers from the water and insert them into each kofta. Place the koftas in the fridge to allow them to firm up (30 minutes is fine, but longer is better).

Now is the time to light your barbecue so it can flame and settle to a nice steady glowing heat.

Sift the flour into a bowl. Add the oil, salt and water and bring it together into a dough. Turn the dough out on to it and knead for 5 minutes until smooth and elastic. If it is too wet and sticky, dust it with a bit more flour as you knead it until it behaves. Divide it into 8 equal pieces and form them into balls. Leave them to rest for 5 minutes.

Mix the yogurt, tahini, lemon juice, cumin and mint together in a small bowl and season to taste with salt.

Remove the koftas from the fridge, brush each one with olive oil and place on the grill of your barbecue. Cook for 4–6 minutes per side until cooked through, being careful not to move them too much.

While the koftas cook, dust a work surface and a rolling pin with flour. Squash the dough balls into fat discs in your palm, then roll them out as thinly as you can into rough circles.

Remove the koftas from the grill and then place the flatbreads on the grill until lightly coloured and starting to blister – about 30 seconds a side. Stack on top of one another to keep them warm while you finish cooking them all.

Serve the koftas with the tahini yogurt and flatbreads. Salad leaves and griddled veg make wonderful accompaniments.

A beloved recipe in our home, Coronation Chicken Salad speaks of spring picnics by the river, while we wait in anticipation for the first trout of the year to be caught on a fly. Garden parties with friends surrounded by roses that are just about to show off their blousy bloom. A very simple dish to knock up that is so useful for spring and summer gatherings and so very different to the overprocessed coronation chicken you find in dreaded plastic tubs on supermarket shelves.

# Coronation Chicken Salad

— SERVES 4 —

1 small red onion, finely sliced
3 tablespoons red wine vinegar
1 tablespoon soft brown sugar
400g (14oz) cooked chicken
    – poached breasts or leftovers
    from a roast are ideal
2 teaspoons garam masala
olive oil
6–8 radishes, cut into a mix
    of slices and wedges
200g (7oz) green beans,
    cooked and cooled
2 celery sticks, thinly sliced
100g (3½oz) mixed salad leaves
50g (1¾oz) flaked almonds,
    toasted
1 teaspoon nigella seeds
1 small bunch of coriander,
    coarsely chopped
10–12 fresh mint leaves,
    thinly sliced
pure sea salt

*For the dressing*
3 tablespoons mango chutney
6 tablespoons yogurt
1 tablespoon mild curry powder
½ garlic clove, finely chopped
juice of 1 lemon

Put the red onion in a small bowl with the vinegar, sugar and a pinch of salt. Mix well until the sugar has dissolved. Leave for at least 15 minutes to pickle and turn pink, the longer the better.

Make the dressing by mixing the mango chutney, yogurt, curry powder and garlic together in a bowl with a pinch of salt and a squeeze of lemon juice. Taste and tweak with more salt and lemon to your liking. If your chutney contains lumps of mango, you can blitz it in a small blender if you like. If your yogurt is particularly thick you may want to thin the dressing down with a dash of hot water to bring it to a spoon-able consistency.

Slice or tear your cooked chicken into pieces and throw them together in a mixing bowl with the garam masala, a pinch of salt and a small dash of oil to help the spices stick. Now mix in the radishes, beans, celery and salad leaves.

You now have the choice between style or speed. If you are feeling artistic, tumble everything in the mixing bowl on to a broad serving plate and spoon the dressing flamboyantly across the top before garnishing with the almonds, seeds and chopped herbs. Remove the onions from their pickling liquid and scatter them across the top. Alternatively, just throw everything apart from the onion pickling liquid into the bowl, mix well and serve.

There is nothing so disappointing as a poorly made pork pie, and as is often the case with most shop-bought pies, disappointment is almost inevitable. Real pork pies are a thing of beauty and well worth the effort that goes into making them. They are not as difficult as you may think – the key is to get yourself organized and not rush, enjoy the gentle process of coaxing the ingredients together to make something magnificent.

# Hand-raised Pork Pies

### — MAKES 5 MEDIUM PIES —

*For the filling*
750g (1lb 10oz) pork mince
250g (9oz) bacon lardons
1 teaspoon freshly
    chopped thyme
1 teaspoon freshly
    chopped sage
1 teaspoon fennel seeds
500ml (18fl oz) chicken
    stock (see page 21)
1 small bunch of thyme
1 garlic clove, bashed
4 leaves of gelatine
pure sea salt and freshly ground
    black pepper

*For the pastry*
200ml (7fl oz) water
270g (9¾oz) lard
670g (1lb 8oz) stoneground
    unbleached white flour,
    plus extra for dusting
1 teaspoon pure sea salt
1 free-range and/or organic
    egg, beaten

To make the filling, mix together the pork, lardons, herbs, 1 teaspoon of salt and 1 teaspoon of pepper. Divide into 5 equal-sized balls and refrigerate.

To make the pastry, melt the water and lard together in a medium saucepan. Put the flour and salt in a mixing bowl and pour in the water and lard mixture. Mix together until there is no dry flour remaining, then knead the mixture on a floured work surface for 2 minutes. Divide into 5 equal-sized balls.

Take 5 water tumblers or pint glasses to use as moulds for the pies. Wrap the glasses with 2 layers of clingfilm to prevent the pastry from sticking. Remove one third of each ball of pastry to use as a lid and set aside covered with a tea towel or clingfilm. Roll out the remaining pastry into thick discs, mould around the base of the glasses and bring the pastry up to roughly 8–10cm (3¼–4in) tall. Turn the glasses upside down to prevent the pastry from slipping down. When each ball of pastry is moulded, place in the fridge for 10 minutes to firm up.

Preheat the oven to 200°C/400°F/gas mark 6.

Remove the pastry from the glasses and place the meatballs in the cavities. Mould the pastry around the meat, stretching the pastry upwards, 1cm (½in) higher than the level of the meat. Roll the pastry lids slightly wider than the pies. Neatly crimp the pastry lids on to the pies. Brush thoroughly with half of the beaten egg and poke a hole in the top of each pie. Bake for 25 minutes. Remove the pies from the oven and brush with more beaten egg, then bake for a further 15 minutes. Leave to cool completely.

Pour the chicken stock into a pan over a low heat, add the thyme, garlic and plenty of salt and pepper and cook for 15 minutes to allow the herbs to infuse. Soak the gelatine in cold water for 10 minutes, then dissolve the leaves in the hot stock. Cool to room temperature.

Gradually pour the stock into the pies through the holes in the top until full, then refrigerate for 1 hour. Top up the stock in the pies if the level has reduced. Return to the fridge to set for 1 hour and serve.

# June

Few things are as lovely as sunrise on the farm in early summer. The air vibrates with warmth and hope and the thrum of life, as insects dance and birds flit in the hazy golden air. The hedgerows trill with nestlings calling for a beakful of caterpillars, while the blossom is everywhere.

Out in the fields we take our first cut of hay and silage, storing it safe for the end of the year. But for now we plan picnics under the oaks, make elderflower cordial from the pollen-laced frothy blooms and soak up these easier days.

This is a really wonderful way to cook a chicken and potatoes, particularly when you're dealing with a properly free-range whole chicken with so much flavour. As it roasts, the potatoes soak up all the garlic- and herb-spiked juices, which often get left in the base of the tin. You end up with the most delicious chicken, which is perfectly suited to the wood oven but also works superbly in a conventional oven too.

# Wood-roast Chicken with Herbs, Potatoes & Aioli

— SERVES 6 —

1.75kg (3lb 13oz) free-range
    chicken
75g (2¾oz) grass-fed butter
4 sprigs of thyme, leaves picked
    and freshly chopped
2 sprigs of marjoram, leaves
    picked and freshly chopped
a large handful of flat-leaf parsley
    leaves, freshly chopped
2 small garlic cloves, grated
1kg (2lb 4 oz) white potatoes,
    peeled and cut into 4–5mm
    (¼in) slices
1 tablespoon extra virgin
    olive oil

*For the aioli*
2 very fresh free-range and/
    or organic egg yolks
2 garlic cloves, grated and
    crushed to a paste
1 teaspoon Dijon mustard
1 tablespoon apple cider
    vinegar or lemon juice
200ml (7fl oz) olive oil
200ml (7fl oz) sunflower oil
pure sea salt and freshly
    ground black pepper

To make the aioli, whisk the egg yolks, garlic, mustard and vinegar and some salt and pepper together in a bowl. Combine the oils in a jug and start to add them in a thin trickle, whisking constantly. When the oils start to emulsify, you can add them a little faster. You should have a thick, glossy, garlicky mayonnaise. If it's too thick, add 1 tablespoon of warm water to loosen it slightly. Set aside until needed.

Pre-fire your wood oven. It should be 200–220°C (400–425°F) when you come to cook. If you are using a conventional oven, preheat it to 180°C/350°F/gas mark 4.

An hour before you are ready to cook, remove the chicken from the fridge to let it come up to room temperature. Place the butter in a bowl and add the thyme, marjoram, parsley, garlic and some salt and pepper. Mix well to combine. Loosen the chicken breast skin a little, easing it away from the flesh with your fingers. Spread the herby butter under the breast skin and all over the chicken.

Place the potatoes in a large bowl with the olive oil and some salt and pepper and tumble together to coat. Scatter in a large roasting tray, in an even layer, and sit the chicken on top. Roast in the oven, turning the tray periodically, for about 30 minutes. Now carefully lift the chicken off the potatoes and give them a quick turn. Replace the bird and return the tray to the oven for a further hour or until the chicken and potatoes are cooked. If you're cooking in the wood oven, check the oven temperature from time to time; if it falls below 120°C (250°F), build up the fire with fresh wood to keep it hot.

To check whether the chicken is cooked, slide the tray to the front of the oven and pull at a leg – it should come away easily. Or use a digital probe thermometer in the thickest part (inside of the thigh, next to the body) to check the core temperature has reached 72°C (162°F). Remove from the oven once cooked. Leave the chicken to rest somewhere warm for 15–20 minutes before carving and serving with the potatoes, aioli and a crisp green salad.

A delicious twist on the classic beef carpaccio. Here, we have used pig's heart in place of fillet steak and a stunning British ewe's milk cheese: Berkswell. Berkswell is sweet and nutty, with a hint of caramel and a definite tang on the finish and similar in style to pecorino. It is made at the aptly named, sixteenth-century Ram Hall in the Heart of England and is one of the finest farmhouse cheeses in the country.

# Seared Pig's Hearts with Berkswell, Fennel & Lovage

— SERVES 2 —

1 litre (1¾ pints) water
50g (1¾oz) pure sea salt
2 pig's hearts
olive oil
juice of 1 lemon
½ fennel bulb, very finely sliced
a small bunch of lovage,
    roughly chopped
    (alternatively use celery
    leaves or flat-leaf parsley)
100g (3½oz) Berkswell or
    pecorino cheese, shaved
a pinch of pure sea salt and
    freshly ground black pepper

Make a brine by whisking together the water and salt until the salt has fully dissolved.

Prepare the hearts by slicing them into quarters lengthways and trimming out any ventricles or bits of sinew.

Place the hearts into a small, non-reactive container (plastic or ceramic), pour over the brine and set aside in the fridge overnight.

The next day, drain the brine away and pat the hearts dry.

Preheat a heavy-based frying pan over a high heat until scorching hot. Lightly dress the hearts with oil and sear very heavily for 1 minute on each side. It's important to get some really good colour on the hearts, so press down using a pair of tongs. Once nicely seared, set the hearts aside to rest for 5 minutes.

Finely slice the hearts and lay out on plates in the style of a carpaccio. Squeeze the lemon over the top and dress with the fennel, lovage leaves and cheese. Drizzle with a good glug of olive oil and season with a good pinch of salt and pepper.

# The Slow Disappearance
# of Family Farms

---

Here's an unsettling statistic: the classic British family farm could die out in the next 30 years if farming continues in its current direction towards bigger, more intensive and fewer farms. According to Defra, farms of less than 100 hectares (247 acres) have halved in number in the last six decades. Smallholdings – farms typically under 50 acres in size – have seen a dramatic decrease too, from about 160,000 in 1950 to less than 30,000 in 2020.

This collapse in family farms has in part been driven by the rise of concentrated animal feeding operations (CAFOs). These mega-farms are industrial farming units where pigs, cows and chickens are crammed by the thousand into rows of warehouse-like buildings or grassless pens. Many units are semi-automated, with feeding run by computer, and only periodic visits by workers. Their presence in the UK has increased by 30% in the past few years alone.

Industrial farming dominates animal production and has an outsized influence on crop growing and land usage. The UK is now home to about 800 mega-farms classed as CAFOs, alongside significant numbers of highly geared industrial farms that are not far off the CAFO status. The result is that huge numbers of industrial farms are taking up equally huge swathes of British land – once home to a tapestry of smaller farms.

With that scale comes the ultimate aim – an ability to reduce costs to please supermarket buyers. This race to the bottom drags small-scale farmers with it – placing them under relentless pressure to make food cheaper and cheaper. And cheap food culture is a force to be reckoned with in the UK; when looking at the amount of income each household spends on food, we come third last in the world. This singular focus has meant we have lost sight of the true cost of our

agricultural model. The cost to our environment. The cost to human health. Even the cost of our land, making access more and more difficult for new farmers to start up enterprises.

Many farmers have not been able to sustain a working farm and have instead jumped off the treadmill and sold out to developers who have covered Grade A farmland that could be producing outstanding food in housing developments. This has further driven up the price of land and made it more scarce and more difficult for the small family farm to survive. 'Dispersal sale' is one of the saddest terms in farming, where livestock, tractors, tools and feed are sold off, as another farmer can take no more. With that sale goes generations of skill, stories and graft, as another family's guardianship of a corner of the British countryside evaporates.

Family farms are what we know. Growing up on a small mixed farm in Kent in the 1960s we were surrounded by fellow family farmers rearing animals and tending crops alongside nature in a community that hummed with life. In 1987, after we'd started our own farming journey on an 1,800-acre hill farm in Wensleydale, we returned to the family farm in Kent, to discover the direction had changed to one of raising half a million chickens a year in an industrial set-up. Worse still, all those neighbouring small family farms had gone. There was nothing. Realizing this ever-more intensive style of farming wasn't the path we wanted to take, we set about building something different. In deepest Devon we found the rural farming community still there, but only just. Many were hanging on by their fingernails. After looking at close to 100 holdings in six months, we eventually bought a 52-acre farm in Devon and named it Pipers Farm. Having seen the sad fading of human presence, life and

*With the sale of each small farm goes generations of skill, stories and graft, as another family's guardianship of a corner of the British countryside evaporates.*

community from the Kent countryside galvanized in us a determination to build a business that would help to sustain the fabric of the community by breathing life back into the rural economy.

Yet Devon is not that far from Kent today. Many of the fellow farmers in our valley are in the global rat race of trying to compete on distorted global prices. We offer an opportunity to change that. What we're doing is trying to redraft the food and farming model with a completely different perspective.

It shouldn't be about bigger and bigger quantities. We want farmers to be able to produce a sustainable amount of food that reaches a customer who respects and appreciates the value of it, so that the farmer gets a fair price for their efforts. Every time a customer buys a piece of meat, they are putting cash straight into small-scale family farms, into communities, and not some anonymous board of investors so they can buy that second home.

By focusing on each individual farm and what those pastures, meadows and copses are best at supporting, be it pastured pigs eating fodder beet crops in rotation with turkeys, or sheep foraging on the Dartmoor hills, we are able

to support these businesses in diversifying their operations and provide a guaranteed and simple route to market, so they can invest for the long term. It's based on handshakes, trust and respect. And it's proof that when it comes to farming, bigger isn't necessarily better.

To have environmental sustainability you need to have economic sustainability. Small family farms want to protect their soil, build biodiversity, protect waterways, they want to because they are engaged with nature, they know their fields, trees, soil, livestock and hedgerows intimately. If they can earn a fair income from farming, they can protect all that. By buying direct from farmers in this way, money is going back into the community. It is helping us to ensure we are able to farm in a way that tackles the climate crisis, regenerating rather than depleting our soil. It is funding projects such as laying down new hedgerows, planting trees, improving water cycles and converting to renewable energy. It's allowing artisan skills to thrive in rural communities, providing links to low-throughput abattoirs and local feed mills. Your support is securing a future for small-scale family farms, and there isn't a second home in sight.

Good baba ganoush takes a bit of time and care to make. When charring the aubergine, cook it until it's done and then cook it some more – you're looking for a texture that's glossy and soft. The aubergine should be deeply charred and completely tender. Our top tip when mixing it all together is to slowly emulsify the olive oil with the tahini and aubergine mixture in order to give it a really creamy texture.

# Fire-cooked Lamb Meatballs with Baba Ganoush & Feta

— SERVES 2 —

**For the baba ganoush**
1 aubergine
2 garlic cloves,
    finely chopped
juice of 1 lemon
3 teaspoons tahini
olive oil
pure sea salt

**For the meatballs**
250g (9oz) grass-fed
    lamb mince
a small handful of mint
    leaves, freshly chopped
a small bunch of flat-leaf
    parsley, freshly chopped
zest of 1 lemon
½ teaspoon fennel
    seeds, crushed
½ teaspoon coriander
    seeds, crushed
¼ teaspoon paprika
½ teaspoon garlic powder
a good pinch of pure sea salt
olive oil

**To serve**
a small handful of
    pumpkin seeds
1 teaspoon ancho chilli flakes
125g (4½oz) feta
a small handful of mint
    leaves, freshly chopped
a small bunch of flat-leaf
    parsley, freshly chopped
extra virgin olive oil,
    for drizzling

Fill the bottom of your barbecue with sustainable lumpwood charcoal and light. Allow the coals to heat until they form a grey coat, then add a few small logs to create a bit more smoke.

For the baba ganoush, place the aubergine over the fire and completely blacken the outside. While the outside is charring, the inside should be becoming gloriously soft and juicy. This will take about 20–30 minutes, depending on how hot your fire is.

Once the outside is puckered and has blistered beautifully, scoop the flesh out of the aubergine and place in a mixing bowl. Roughly mix the aubergine with the garlic, lemon juice and some salt. Blitz the tahini and a little olive oil together and then pour into the mixing bowl, combining with the aubergine to make a smooth and glossy baba ganoush. Set aside while you cook the lamb.

In a mixing bowl, combine the lamb mince with the herbs, lemon zest, spices and salt and mix well. Roll the lamb mixture into small balls. Drizzle some oil into a hot, heavy-based frying pan and fry the meatballs for 5–10 minutes or until golden on the outside. Remove from the pan and set aside. Add the pumpkin seeds and chilli flakes to the pan and toast for a few minutes. There should be a gloriously meaty, nutty, spicy smell coming from the hot pan.

To serve, spread the baba ganoush over 2 plates, then layer the lamb meatballs on top with the crumbled feta, toasted pumpkin seeds, chilli flakes, chopped herbs and a drizzle of extra virgin olive oil.

The sweet nectarines are the perfect foil for the charred, herby chicken. They are easier to prepare and cook if they are a little underripe; they'll eventually yield and soften in the heat. Marinating the chicken is great if you have the time, but if not you can finish it with a squeeze of lemon juice and a few fresh thyme leaves instead.

# Griddled Chicken Thighs
# with Pesto & Nectarine Salad

— SERVES 4 —

8 free-range boneless
    chicken thighs
6 nectarines, halved and pitted
80g (2¾oz) mixed salad leaves
1 ball of burrata or mozzarella
pure sea salt and freshly
    ground black pepper

*For the marinade*
1 lemon
1 small bunch of thyme
3 garlic cloves, skin on
olive oil
a pinch of pure sea salt

*For the pesto*
60g (2¼oz) pine nuts,
    lightly toasted
30g (1oz) basil
4 tablespoons olive oil

Peel the zest from the lemon with a veg peeler in long strips. Bash the thyme, garlic cloves and lemon zest together in a pestle and mortar. Juice the lemon. Mix everything together with the chicken thighs in a shallow tray with a dash of olive oil and a pinch of salt. Leave to marinate in the fridge for at least 1 hour, ideally overnight. Remove the chicken from the fridge at least 20 minutes before cooking.

Light the barbecue and let the charcoal get to a nice steady heat. Alternatively, put a griddle pan on the hob over a medium–high heat.

Remove the thighs from the marinade and season generously. Place them skin-side down and cook for 15–20 minutes, turning every so often, until nicely coloured on both sides.

After the chicken has been cooking for about 10 minutes, lightly brush the nectarines with some oil. Place them on the barbecue too (or into a frying pan on the hob) and griddle them, face-side down, over a medium heat until nicely marked. This should take 4–5 minutes; resist the temptation to play with them too much or they'll tend to stick or tear. Flip them and cook for a further 4 minutes or so until softened. Remove the chicken and nectarines and leave them to one side to rest and cool for at least 15 minutes.

Meanwhile, to make the pesto, bash half the pine nuts together in a pestle and mortar with the basil and a pinch of salt until you have a paste. Work in the olive oil. Alternatively, you could whizz it all together in a small blender.

To serve, slice the chicken into generous strips and cut the nectarines into clumsy wedges. Tumble them together with the salad leaves on a serving plate and then tear the burrata or mozzarella across the top. Spoon over the pesto and garnish with the remaining pine nuts. Finish with a little pinch of salt and pepper.

With simplicity at the heart of this recipe, it just shows you what a handful of good ingredients lovingly tended to can deliver. Light on process but big on flavour, after just a few simple steps you have a really special meal on your plate. The key to success is making sure you carefully render the lamb fat down on each chop so you end up with a piece of meat that is beautifully caramelized and ready to take up all the flavour from the aromatic accompaniments.

# Lamb Chops with Roast Aubergine, Yogurt, Tahini & Za'atar

— SERVES 2 —

1 aubergine
olive oil
juice of 1 lemon
2 tablespoons za'atar
a small handful of
    coriander, freshly chopped,
    plus extra leaves to serve
1 tablespoon light tahini
200g (7oz) yogurt
4 lamb chops
pure sea salt and freshly
    ground black pepper

Preheat the oven to 200°C/400°F/gas mark 6.

Cut the aubergine into large chunks, scatter over some salt and leave to stand for 15 minutes.

Transfer the aubergine to a roasting tray, drizzle with olive oil and roast for 20 minutes until golden and soft.

Prepare a dressing by combining the lemon juice, za'atar (reserving a pinch to sprinkle on the lamb), coriander, 4 tablespoons of olive oil and some salt and pepper. Toss the hot aubergine with the dressing.

Prepare a simple tahini yogurt by combining the tahini with the yogurt and seasoning well with salt and pepper.

Preheat a griddle pan until scorchingly hot. Season the lamb. Place the lamb chops, fat-side down, on the pan and cook until the fat is golden brown and rendered. Then cook the chops for 2 minutes on each side.

Rest the lamb for 5 minutes before serving with the dressed aubergine, tahini yogurt and a final scattering of coriander and za'atar.

Puntarelle is a variant of chicory and has a slightly sharp and bitter taste, which adds another dimension to this flavour-packed dish. If you can't find puntarelle, wild dandelion leaves make a great alternative. The creamy butter beans are the perfect base for the beautifully marbled entrecote steak and rich aioli. This dish is a wonderful option for gathering people together on a warm early summer's evening.

# Entrecote Steak with Butter Beans, Shallots, Puntarelle & Aioli

— SERVES 2 —

olive oil
10 small shallots, halved
500ml (18fl oz) beef stock
    (see page 22)
400g (14oz) can good-quality
    butter beans
1 grass-fed entrecote steak
a knob of unsalted
    grass-fed butter
a big handful of puntarelle
    (or kale if unavailable)
1 small bunch of flat-leaf
    parsley, freshly chopped
pure sea salt and freshly
    ground black pepper

*For the aioli*
2 very fresh free-range
    and/or organic egg yolks
2 garlic cloves, grated,
    then crushed to a paste
1 teaspoon Dijon mustard
1 tablespoon apple cider
    vinegar or lemon juice
200ml (7 fl oz) olive oil
200ml (7 fl oz) sunflower oil

Whisk the egg yolks, garlic, mustard and vinegar and some salt and pepper together in a bowl to combine. Combine the oils in a jug and start to add them in a thin trickle, whisking constantly. When the oil starts to emulsify with the yolks you can add it a little faster. If things have gone to plan you will have a thick, glossy, garlicky mayonnaise. If it's too thick, add 1 tablespoon of warm water to loosen it slightly. Set aside until needed.

Set a heavy-based frying pan over a medium-high heat. Add a little oil and the shallots and fry them for 5–6 minutes until golden on one side. Add the stock and butter beans and reduce until a thick, glossy sauce forms, then set aside.

Heat a separate frying pan over a high heat. Season the steaks with olive oil, salt and pepper. Drizzle a little oil into the pan and fry the steaks in the hot pan for 2 minutes on each side until golden brown. Add a knob of butter and baste the steaks for a further 2–3 minutes, then remove from the heat and leave the steaks to rest for 6 minutes.

Finely chop the puntarelle and wilt into the warm butter bean sauce alongside the parsley.

Spoon the beans into serving bowls, slice the steak and place on top of the beans alongside a generous blob of the aioli.

When the younger family members come to stay, we fire up our handmade pizza oven for a 'build your own pizza night'. Encouraging the younger generation to form a connection with their food is at the heart of our ethos. We believe it is vitally important to get children into the kitchen at a young age to boost their confidence and skills – and what's more fun than making pizzas?

# Sausage, Fennel & Cheddar Pizza with Crispy Sourdough Crumb

## — SERVES 6–8 —

### For the dough
475ml (17fl oz) warm water
4 tablespoons extra
    virgin olive oil
1 tablespoon unbleached
    caster sugar
1 teaspoon fine sea salt
2 x 7g dried yeast sachets
1kg (2lb 4oz) '00' flour, or
    800g (1lb 12oz) stoneground
    unbleached white flour, plus
    extra for dusting

### For the topping
1kg (2lb 4oz) natural pork
    sausage meat
400g (14oz) jar of passata
250g (9oz) clothbound
    mature Cheddar cheese
½ fennel bulb, grated
a few fresh oregano leaves
150g (5½oz) sourdough
    breadcrumbs

To make the dough, add the warm water, oil, sugar, salt and yeast to a jug. Mix together and then leave for a few minutes.

On a clean work surface, create a mound of the flour and in the centre make a little well. Pour the yeast liquid into the well and, with a fork, gradually mix the flour into the liquid. Once the flour is fully combined and you have a dough, give it a good knead until it becomes smooth and elastic. Take a good-sized mixing bowl and dust with flour, place the dough in and cover with a damp cloth. Leave the dough to rest in a warm room for 1–2 hours until it has doubled in size.

Preheat the oven to 250°C/475°F/gas mark 9, or use a pizza oven if you have one.

Remove the dough from the bowl. Dust your work surface with a little flour and give the dough a good knead to push the air out with your hands – this is called knocking back the dough.

The dough can either be used immediately or can be placed in the fridge or freezer to be used another time. If you are making the pizzas straight away, divide the dough up into 6–8 circles, about 5mm (¼in) thick.

Break the sausage meat into small pieces and spread over a small baking dish. Roast in the oven for 15 minutes until cooked through.

If you are using the oven to cook the pizzas, preheat 2 large baking sheets in the oven.

Place a circle of rolled dough on to a hot baking sheet (or cold pizza peel). Quickly top with a smear of the passata, a good sprinkling of Cheddar, some dots of sausage meat, fennel, oregano leaves and breadcrumbs. Bake for 10 minutes in the oven, or if using a pizza oven, turn every 1–2 minutes, and cook for 5–6 minutes. Repeat to make the remaining pizzas.

# July

Moving the cattle in mob grazing herds keeps the grass
stimulated, the pasture productive and the cows happy. Our daily
checks find us lingering to watch their languorous tail-swishing,
as they chew the cud and bask in the shade of the oaks.

The chickens craft little dust baths for themselves, flicking their
feathers and dozing in the sunshine, and in the meadow, summer
orchids are resplendent. Meanwhile, the farmhouse table heaves
with beautiful, colourful food as the kitchen garden and fields
all reach their peak productivity.

# How to Have a Pipers Farm Barbecue

Building a fire, filling the air with the scent of woodsmoke, and cooking something delicious to eat, not only can be so viscerally rewarding but it is the most natural way to cook. After all, humans from across the globe have been cooking in this way for millennia.

The act of cooking over fire is one that cannot be hurried. Wood must be gathered and chopped, or charcoal poured into a pit and lit, patiently waiting for that magical grey coat to form. Before you even begin to cook, humility and restraint must be applied and your senses deployed to judge when the time is right to commence.

By slowing down and breathing in fresh air, cooking outdoors allows us to switch off and unwind.

For us, cooking outdoors is a way to really celebrate the connection between the food we are eating and the surroundings in which we live. There is a sense of freedom, a feeling of space and openness, perhaps even mindfulness, and a kinship with nature.

We are lucky to have access to our own wild land to cook from, but you don't need much space in order to enjoy the smoky satisfaction that cooking outdoors brings. A small garden, park, beach or picnic spot can all provide the same joy. These days there are all sorts of environmentally friendly, safe and portable barbecues that can be taken with you on adventures. On that note, you don't need a load of complicated kit, in fact, we would advise the simpler the better. A pit, a grill, some fuel, matches and a good knife are really all that's required.

When it comes to serving up a meal cooked al fresco there is often a lot of focus on the meat element, much bravado and complexity seem to surround the heady world of barbecuing. While not turning your meat into a charred relic is important, it is also equally crucial to provide plenty of seasonal salads and sides to give you respite from the intensity of meat cooked over flame. Seasonal veg, herbs and leaves are essential tools in our armoury to make a barbecued feast really special. The fresh or earthy flavours change the palate and make that juicy steak or slow-cooked lamb shoulder taste all the better.

Like many avid fire cookery fans, we cook over flames all year round, even being known to pull one of our firepits into the farmhouse kitchen in the depths of winter. Fire cooking doesn't just have to be an activity for fair weather, it is simply a wonderful way to celebrate real food and hands-on cookery.

You should be able to taste the terroir, the grassy, earthy flavours that perfume slow-grown, pasture-fed lamb. Ageing the carcass, for say, two weeks, only enhances the delicate flavour and improves the texture. Even when it comes to mince, the difference is remarkable – and that's the secret ingredient in these sensationally smoky burgers.

# Lamb Burgers with Smoky Harissa Aubergines & Tahini Mayo

## — SERVES 4 —

2 teaspoons black peppercorns
2 teaspoons cumin seeds
2 teaspoons coriander seeds
500g (1lb 2oz) grass-fed
    lamb mince
2 teaspoons nigella seeds
4 garlic cloves, crushed
1 medium aubergine
4 burger buns, halved
1 teaspoon chipotle chilli flakes
1 tablespoon olive oil
pure sea salt and freshly
    ground black pepper

*For the harissa*
4–5 large red chillies
1 teaspoon coriander seeds
½ teaspoon cumin seeds
4 garlic cloves, sliced
½ teaspoon pure sea salt
a squeeze of lemon juice
2 teaspoons tomato purée
1 tablespoon olive oil,
    plus extra to store

*For the mayonnaise*
4 tablespoons mayonnaise
1 tablespoon tahini
zest and juice of ½ lemon
1 small garlic clove, grated

Prepare your fire. You want a hot bed of glowing embers.

To make the harissa, carefully lay the chillies directly on top of the hot embers and cook, turning often, until the skins blacken and the flesh is tender. Place the cooked chillies in a bowl, cover and leave to cool completely. Peel off the blackened skins, split the chillies open, then scrape out the seeds with a knife and discard them.

Toast the coriander and cumin seeds in a dry frying pan for a minute or so, then crush them coarsely with a pestle and mortar. Add the chillies, garlic and salt and bash until you have a fragrant paste. Stir in the lemon juice, tomato purée and olive oil. Set aside.

To make the burgers, place a small pan over a medium heat. Add the peppercorns, cumin and coriander seeds and toast gently for 3–4 minutes. Tip the contents of the pan into a pestle and mortar and grind to a fairly fine texture. Place the lamb mince in a large bowl. Add the ground spices, nigella seeds, garlic and some salt and pepper. Combine the mix thoroughly, mixing it for 2–3 minutes to help it bind. Shape the seasoned mince into 4 equal-sized burgers.

Combine the mayonnaise with the tahini, lemon zest and juice and garlic and set aside.

Slice the aubergine into 1–2cm-(½–¾in-)thick rounds. Turn the slices through 2 tablespoons of harissa so they're nicely coated. Lay the aubegine slices down over a medium–hot area of the fire and cook for 6–8 minutes on each side. Keep warm.

When you're ready to cook the burgers, make sure the fire is super-hot to ensure they take on lots of colour and stay juicy. Lay the burgers carefully on the grill – they should start to sizzle and smoke immediately. Cook for 3–4 minutes on each side.

To serve, pop a burger into each bun, top with a few slices of smoky aubergine, a generous spoonful of tahini mayo, a scattering of chilli flakes, a drizzle of olive oil and finish with a dash of harissa.

This versatile marinade can be used for other barbecue favourites, not just luscious lamb. It works so well with native breed pork, properly reared chicken and even sustainable fish. A quick and simple marinade to have in your repertoire for when the weather is kind and evenings are stretched out with the scent of barbecue smoke wafting around the neighbourhood and the comforting sounds of clinking glasses and laughter fill the air.

# Fire-cooked Lamb Leg Steaks with Fennel & Thyme

— SERVES 3–4 —

2 large garlic cloves, grated
zest of 1 large lemon
1 teaspoon chilli flakes
2 tablespoons fennel seeds, coarsely crushed
2 tablespoons olive oil
6 lamb leg steaks, weighing about 700–800g (1lb 9oz–1lb 12oz), about 2–3cm (¾–1¼in) thick
1 small bunch of woody thyme sprigs
a handful of fennel fronds (if available)
pure sea salt and freshly ground black pepper

Combine the garlic, lemon zest, chilli flakes, fennel seeds, olive oil and some salt and pepper. Rub half this mixture all over the lamb steaks. Cover and leave to marinate for a few hours if you can.

Fill the bottom of your barbecue with sustainable lumpwood charcoal and light. Allow the coals to heat until they form a grey coat, then add a few small logs to create a bit more smoke.

Place the lamb carefully down on the grill (it should begin sizzling instantly) and cook for 3–4 minutes on the first side, spooning any remaining lemony, garlicky marinade over the meat. As you turn the lamb over, arrange the thyme and fennel fronds around the meat. They will begin to crackle and smoke a little, but don't worry about this. It all amounts to flavour.

Cook the lamb on the second side for 3–4 minutes. If at any point the meat seems to be colouring too much or the fire flares up, remove it and allow the flames to die back before replacing on the grill over the embers.

Remove the lamb and leave it to rest for 6–8 minutes before serving with a simple array of summery salads and breads.

Cooking over fire is all about managing heat. There is a connection between the cook and the flames that requires you to use all your senses in coaxing your ingredients along, moving from direct heat when you want a little char flavour, to indirect to avoid burning your ingredients to a crisp. It is for this reason we love cooking over fire, it reconnects us in a mindful way to our basic human instincts.

# Fire-cooked Spatchcock Chicken with Lemon, Marjoram, Black Pepper & Garlic

— SERVES 4 —

1 free-range chicken,
    weighing about 1.2–1.5kg
    (2lb 10oz–3lb 5oz)
a handful of marjoram leaves
25g (1oz) grass-fed butter,
    softened
zest of 1 lemon
1 garlic clove, finely grated
a selection of other fresh
    green herbs, for cooking
pure sea salt and freshly
    ground black pepper

Remove the chicken from the fridge at least 2–3 hours before you intend to cook it.

When you are ready to cook, place the chicken breast-side down on a chopping board. Using a pair of kitchen scissors, cut down each side of the backbone and remove it. Open the bird out so it's nice and flat – it'll cook much more evenly this way.

Chop the marjoram relatively finely and place in a bowl with the butter, lemon zest, garlic, a good pinch of salt and plenty of black pepper. Rub the bird all over with the soft herby butter and, if you can, try and get some under the skin of the breast. Sprinkle the whole bird with a little more salt and pepper.

Light your barbecue. When the flames have burned back and you have a good bed of medium–hot coals, it's time to cook the chicken.

Place the chicken on the barbecue, cut-side down, breast-side up, scatter over half the additional herbs and cook gently for about 45–50 minutes. Make sure the heat isn't too fierce or you'll burn the chicken before it's cooked through. You may need to move the embers of the barbecue around or raise/lower the height of the grill to find the optimum heat for this kind of gentle cooking.

Once you've cooked the first side, carefully turn the chicken over, scatter over the remaining herbs and grill on the breast side for a further 20–30 minutes or until the juices run clear and the bird is cooked through.

Leave the chicken to rest for at least 10 minutes before serving. Carve and serve with flatbreads (see page 108) and a leafy herby salad.

# What Does Good Farming Look Like?

---

Beyond the hedges and farm gates of our countryside lies an invisible domain of activity mysterious to most. Farming is an opaque world to the average consumer, but as all rivers run to the sea, all food leads back to the soil, and ultimately impacts the planet in ways that scientists are still getting to grips with.

The tricky thing about farming is that it is a milieu of complicated moving parts sitting within the already wildly intricate tangle of nature. Farming is affected by the weather, people, policy, politics, economics and history. What was farmed in a field in previous years will impact soil nutrient content, or parasite populations. Layer over the often unpredictable ecological interactions of nature, from pests and predators to drought and deluge, along with climate change, and you have a intensely tricky thing to understand and manage.

So how do we find farming that does good? Let's start with a field of barley. That field could be a few acres dotted with trees, in countryside woven with a mosaic of habitats of ancient hedgerows, ponds and rough grass pasture, fertilized with clover leys and farmyard manure; or it could be 15,000 acres of monoculture that runs far beyond the horizon. Flat and hedge-free, the latter is easy to harvest with ever-bigger machinery and managed with chemical fertilizers and pesticides which can be bought in a few clicks. Or take a herd of beef cattle – on one farm the cows may be moved around a small mixed farm, stimulating pasture growth, eating a diverse diet of grasses and meadow herbs that need only sunshine and rain to grow, promoting biodiversity through the rich manure they leave behind. Compare that to a herd that is kept in fenced 'feedlots' bare of pasture, where chemical fertilizer-fuelled soya is trucked to the trough, from increasingly land-hungry farming systems.

Admittedly these are oversimplified comparisons, but the point is this – all types of farming are in conflict with nature, but in each of the previous comparisons one method is in a much greater conflict with nature than the other. The monoculture and beef feedlot systems are one-way streets. The model is linear; put something in one end, take a lot out of the other, and externalize the costs. The mixed farm is far more circular, with the nutrients and energy contained in the system.

The lowest-impact farming uses nature as an ally in this way, instead of viewing it as an inconvenience that needs to be removed before farming can take place. Nature's aim is to fill every niche and corner of our planet with life. From fungi to forest, skies to soil, sea to river, pasture to plains, the way that each species affects and is affected by its neighbouring creatures and environment is mind-boggling. The very best farming embraces nature as part of its existence and mimics it.

Using natural manures to fertilize the soil rather than artificially produced nitrogen is a prime example. That is how nature renews itself. In nature you would never get acres of a single species in the way you find in a monoculture, as myriad other species of wildlife would dilute dominance in a constant succession of growth and competition. It is part of the root of the arable struggle against pests and fungal diseases – they rip through unchecked without a diverse bank of other species to respond and keep them in check, as is nature's way.

In contrast, farming systems that avoid this specialization at all levels come closer to how nature behaves. Intercropping uses diversity of crops and companion plantings to deter pests, silvopasture combines trees that produce wood or crops with livestock grazing, while agroforestry is a way of boosting the productivity

*The lowest-impact farming uses nature as an ally, instead of viewing it as an inconvenience that needs to be removed.*

of a piece of land by mixing trees with other layers of crops.

Certified farming systems such as organic and pasture fed have attempted to guide consumers through this complexity. Over the years, more and more types of farming have appeared, which tends to muddy the waters in many ways, though the intention is no doubt good to start off with. The trouble is that when you label a type of farming it immediately becomes divisive. Is one really better than the others? That's the difficult part. Going back to the myriad moving parts to any farming system and how it interacts with and influences nature, it is impossible to define and audit every element. What should we focus on? Is it earthworms per square metre of soil, chemical run-off per acre or bird species diversity per holding? Is the better farmer the one who produces the most food per acre, or the one with the most invertebrate biodiversity?

It gets harder to find clarity when marketing machines rootle their way into the mix. 'Regenerative farming' sounds like a positive, all-encompassing term that denotes a circular economy model of farming which feeds nature

and breathes life back into the countryside. However, in many ways it is dangerous, as there is no agreed definition of the term, so it is open to abuse by unscrupulous marketers who splash it about to push profit.

Our view is that the best farming mixes the old with the new. Small-scale family farms which use minimal inputs, that grow crops and livestock in a rotation where one feeds the other are best placed to renew nature and protect the countryside while producing truly great food. These farmers know each field by name, they know the land and have an intimate relationship with the soil. These farming relationships are based on trust, community, the local economy and local jobs. The anonymization of the food chain has left it open to abuse. The commercialization of farming, where it became about a march to scale, specialization and profit above all else, has been its undoing. We forgot we were growing food to nourish ourselves and enjoy. Here at Pipers Farm we have steadily ploughed our own furrow in the other direction, in a system that has people and place at its heart. That's truly the greatest farming of all.

We hesitate to call this a straight Caesar salad as it is cluttered with all kinds of veg that would never appear in the original; all flashed across the barbecue alongside free-range chicken breasts for a wonderfully smoky finish. The dressing is pretty faithful though, with plenty of pungent garlic, salty anchovy and sharp lemon.

# Chicken with Summer Veg Salad & Caesar Dressing

— SERVES 4 —

2 free-range chicken breasts,
    skin on
3 small lettuces, each cut
    into 8 wedges
150g (5½oz) green beans
2 courgettes, cut in
    half lengthways
150g (5½oz) radishes
olive oil
200g (7oz) sourdough,
    cut into croutons
100g (3½oz) garden peas
a piece of hard cheese, grated
pure sea salt and freshly
    ground black pepper
1 bunch of parsley, finely
    chopped, to garnish
8 wooden barbecue skewers
    (soaked in water to stop
    them burning)

*For the dressing*
1 garlic clove
2 salted anchovy fillets,
    chopped
1 free-range and/or organic
    egg yolk
½ tablespoon Dijon mustard
juice of 1 lemon
5 tablespoons olive oil

Mix the garlic, anchovies, egg yolk and mustard together in a bowl with 1 tablespoon of lemon juice. Whisk in the oil, a little at a time, until you have a dressing the consistency of a thick yogurt; if it seems a bit too thick, thin it down with a dash of boiling water. Taste and adjust with salt and lemon juice.

Remove the chicken from the fridge at least 20 minutes before cooking. Light your barbecue and let your wood or coals get to a nice medium–high heat.

Meanwhile, lightly brush all the veg with olive oil and season lightly with salt. Thread the radishes and croutons on to skewers, so you can turn them easily without having to chase them around with your tongs. Brush the croutons with olive oil too, and season with salt.

Place the skewers on the cooler barbecue edges where the heat is less fierce and turn them every couple of minutes until the croutons are crisp and golden and the radishes still have a slight bite to them.

Season the chicken generously with salt and pepper and place it, skin-side down, over the high heat. Cook for 6–8 minutes, turning every so often, until nicely coloured on both sides. Leave to one side to rest for at least 5 minutes.

Cook the veg alongside the chicken – veg by veg or fill the grill with everything at once if space allows. The lettuce wedges need 1 minute each side until lightly wilted and charred. The green beans will take a couple of minutes until softened and slightly blistered. The courgettes will take about 2 minutes a side until starting to soften.

Throw the lettuce wedges and green beans into a large mixing bowl, slice the courgettes into interestingly angled pieces and add these too, along with the peas. Slide the radishes and croutons off the skewers straight into the bowl. Slice the chicken and throw it into the bowl with half the dressing. Mix well and pile it on to a serving dish. Spoon over the remaining dressing and finish by shaving some hard cheese across the top with a veg peeler. Garnish with some parsley.

Artichokes have been eaten for millennia. While more commonly found in the Mediterranean, they do grow well in the UK, with the main harvest from June onward. They are striking plants, large and architectural with serrated silvery leaves and purple flowers, making them an excellent pit stop for bees. For many of us, artichokes are little more than vehicles for molten butter or, even better, dollops of homemade mayonnaise. However, there is so much more that can be gained from them – they pair perfectly with gloriously fatty pork chops. This stunning combination of pork, artichokes and anchovies will quickly become a summer favourite.

# Fire-cooked Pork Chops with Artichokes & Anchovies

## — SERVES 2 —

2 native breed pork chops
1 teaspoon Saddleback lard
1 tablespoon grass-fed butter
3 globe artichokes, peeled, choke removed and halved
1 garlic clove, crushed
2 anchovies
a few sage leaves
1 lemon, halved
pure sea salt

Fill the bottom of your barbecue with sustainable lumpwood charcoal. Light the coals and allow them to heat up and develop a grey coat.

Generously season the pork chops with salt. Take a cast-iron frying pan and place it over the fire. Once it is smoking hot, add the lard to the pan, followed by the pork chops. Cook on one side for about 4 minutes until the pork is caramelized. Turn the chops over and add the butter, artichokes, garlic, anchovies, sage and lemon to the pan.

At this point, everything should be browning gloriously. With a spoon, break the anchovies down into the foaming butter and use it to baste the chops and artichokes for a further 3–4 minutes.

Remove the chops from the pan and leave to rest on the side while you continue to cook the artichokes in the butter over a gentle heat for a further 5 minutes, or until softened.

Squeeze the cooked lemon over the artichokes and serve.

This innovative take on a surf and turf is easy to make and even easier to eat. Tacos are perfect for al fresco summer cooking on a beach, with the lapping waves providing the ideal dinnertime soundtrack.

# Bavette Steak & Lobster Tacos with Pickled Samphire

## — SERVES 8 —

1 small bag of fresh seaweed, washed
800g–1kg (1lb 12oz–2lb 4oz) uncooked Cornish lobster, humanely dispatched
750g (1lb 10oz) grass-fed bavette steak
1 tablespoon olive oil
2 teaspoons cumin seeds, coarsely crushed
½ teaspoon chilli flakes
pure sea salt and freshly ground black pepper

*For the tortillas*
250g (9oz) stoneground unbleached white flour, plus extra for dusting
1 teaspoon baking powder
½ teaspoon pure fine sea salt
110ml (3¾fl oz) water
50ml (2fl oz) sunflower oil

*For the pickled samphire*
100g (3½oz) marsh samphire
2 tablespoons cider vinegar
2 tablespoons unrefined sugar
2 tablespoons freshly chopped coriander
1 green chilli, deseeded and sliced

*To serve*
4 tablespoons soured cream
a handful of mint leaves, freshly chopped
a few chilli flakes (optional)

To make the tortilla dough, place the flour, baking powder and salt in a bowl and whisk to combine. Combine the water and oil and add to the flour. Mix together until it forms a dough. Dust a work surface with flour and knead the dough for a few minutes until smooth and even. Cover and leave it to rest.

Light your barbecue and get a hot fire going. You want a bed of glowing embers giving out a good high heat.

Wrap the seaweed around the lobster to surround the shell so that when you sit it over the fire the steam gets trapped and it cooks more evenly. Grill, turning regularly, for 15–20 minutes or until the shell has changed from blackish blue to orangey red.

Meanwhile, trickle the steak with the olive oil and sprinkle over the cumin seeds and chilli flakes. Season all over with salt and pepper. Lay the steak over a nice hot part of the fire and cook for 3–4 minutes on each side. You want to caramelize the outside, but keep it lovely and juicy in the middle, so don't overdo it.

While the steak and lobster are resting, combine the samphire with the vinegar, sugar and coriander and the green chilli to taste.

Divide the tortilla dough into 8 equal pieces, then shape them into round balls. Roll out the balls on a floured surface until 12–15cm (4½–6in) wide. Set a small, heavy frying pan over the fire. When it's hot, start cooking the tortillas, one at a time. Lay them into the pan and cook for 45 seconds–1 minute on each side or until they are beginning to take on spots of colour.

To serve, split the lobster and remove the meat from the tail. Crack the claws and pick out the meat. Cut the steak across the grain into slices about 1–2 cm (½–¾in) thick. Lay a few strips of steak down on a warm tortilla. Pile on a small handful of lobster and top with some samphire. Spoon over a little soured cream and finish with fresh mint leaves and a pinch of extra chilli flakes, if you like.

# August

The lush growth of high summer sees nature almost collapse in on itself with abundance on the farm. Hedgerows are heavy with leaf, flower and fern, and sleepy after the exuberant growth of the past few months. Seeds set, second broods of wild birds fledge, and we ready ourselves for harvest time.

If the weather is kind, we bring in crops for winter feed – barley and oats. It's dusty, dirty work, but gathering round a table on a summer evening over good food and drink makes these some of the most fulfilling days. With one eye on the months ahead, now is the time for preserving – damson jam, apple chutney and cucumber pickle to fill the larder.

When you're faced with a glut of summer tomatoes and courgettes you need a variety of dishes up your sleeve to celebrate the season's abundance. This delicious lamb dish is such a brilliant thing to eat at this time of year to help you make a dent in your summer harvest. The young, twisting tendrils of agretti provide a lovely crunch to this salad, bringing a salty, minerally flavour that works so well with properly reared grass-fed lamb.

# Rack of Lamb with Courgettes, Tomatoes, Goat's Curd & Agretti

— SERVES 2 —

300g (10½oz) grass-fed rack of lamb
olive oil
500g (1lb 2oz) heritage tomatoes
2 small courgettes, finely sliced
a small bunch of agretti or samphire, tough stalks discarded
a drizzle of cider vinegar
100g (3½oz) goat's curd or feta cheese
pure sea salt and freshly ground black pepper

Preheat the oven to 200°C/400°F/gas mark 6.

Season the lamb well with olive oil, salt and pepper. Place a heavy-based frying pan over a medium heat, add a drizzle of oil, then add the lamb, fat-side down. Gently cook to render the lamb fat until golden and crispy – this will take a minimum of 15 minutes.

Transfer the lamb to a roasting tray and place in the oven for 8 minutes. Remove from the oven and leave to rest for 10 minutes.

While the lamb is resting, prepare the salad. Chop the tomatoes into bite-sized pieces and place in a large bowl with the courgettes and agretti. Drizzle with olive oil and cider vinegar, season with salt and pepper and toss to combine the ingredients.

Carve the lamb and season with more salt and pepper if necessary. Serve the lamb cutlets alongside the salad, dotted with blobs of the goat's curd.

As impressive as this dish looks, it is rather uncomplicated. Using the heat from the fire, baby beetroots are rendered into soft submission. Bavette steak needs very little encouragement to become sensational; a flame and a good pinch of salt are really all it takes. The fresh horseradish sauce is a doddle, you'll find yourself whipping this up often when beef is planned for the table.

# Fire-cooked Bavette Steak with Ember-roast Beetroots & Lovage

— SERVES 4 —

1 small bunch of baby beetroots
750g (1lb 10oz) grass-fed
    bavette steak
a splash of vintage cider vinegar
a drizzle of extra virgin olive oil
a small handful of fresh lovage
    or marjoram or oregano
pure sea salt

*For the horseradish sauce*
½ small horseradish root
a dollop of crème frâiche
a squeeze of lemon juice

In the base of your barbecue pour in half a standard bag of sustainable lumpwood charcoal, set alight and wait until the coals have developed a thick grey coat.

Place the baby beetroots in the outer embers of a fire and leave to cook for about 40 minutes until charred and tender, turning every now and then to ensure they cook evenly.

To make the horseradish sauce, finely grate the fresh horseradish root and mix with the crème frâiche, tasting as you go so as not to lose the fieriness of the horseradish. Season with a good pinch of salt and a squeeze of lemon juice.

When the beetroots are almost ready, season the bavette generously with salt and allow it to penetrate. Place the bavette over the fire and leave it to char for about 5 minutes. Once a beautiful brown (not black) crust has formed, flip the steak over and cook on the other side for about 4 minutes. Turn back over and cook for a further 3–4 minutes. You want to take the steak to medium-rare.

Remove the steak from the heat and leave to rest while you season the beetroots with salt and a little cider vinegar.

Thinly slice the steak against the grain and serve in a bowl with the beetroots and horseradish. Finish with a sprinkle of lovage and a good drizzle of olive oil.

# What We Eat Shapes the World We Live In

———

Learning how to cook, how to feed a family, nourish ourselves and show our feelings through food runs deep into the psyche, into the primitive brain. It's where human identity, culture, tradition and connection to the land live, because there was a time when we knew where all our food came from, and exactly how it was grown and reared. Food was deeply entwined with our sense of place in the world, part of the human condition of knowing who we are. Special ingredients were sought out as they appeared with the seasons or were grown with pride, then consumed and shared with reverence. This is why when people emigrate to new countries, cooking food from their own cultures, using handed-down recipes, techniques and ingredients, is so significant. They are saying, 'I am here'. It is because of this deep connection that perhaps the most potent facet of food lies in our feelings about who taught us to cook and the food philosophies that underpin what we do in the kitchen.

The cookery and butchery that inform the principles of Pipers Farm are rooted in these same connected beginnings. It was everyday farmhouse kitchen activity that was commonplace up until the 1980s, modest veg and slow-grown meat moving into the kitchen from the veg garden, hedgerow-lined fields, rainswept livestock and clay-rich soil. We had to wait for meat and ate it sparingly, stretching it across as many meals as possible and respecting the animal by using every scrap. This was before the advent of cheap and accessible convenience food from globally traded, industrially reared meat which made grounded, traditional family farming seem irrelevant as it sat outside the system.

Meat and grain have been traded as global commodities for centuries, but today the scale is mind-boggling, with livestock and crops being moved on the Futures Markets before they have even been planted or conceived. This system gives industrial-scale farmers a price for their goods ahead of time so they can plan cashflow and farm investments. However, turning a locally produced animal or crop into a global commodity removes any incentive to care for the animal or the land in a way that comes at a cost. The wheat, beef, corn or poultry is anonymized once it enters the international system, and so doing anything above the bare minimum required to produce it simply isn't reflected in what farmers are paid for the food.

*Turning a locally produced animal or crop into a global commodity removes any incentive to care for the animal or the land in a way that comes at a cost.*

And that's the key – cheap meat doesn't reflect the true cost of producing it. Managing lower numbers of native breed grass-fed livestock in balance with nature doesn't pollute waterways, use carbon-hungry agrochemicals or flown-in feed that drives deforestation. Intensive farms are forced to feed their livestock antibiotics to keep diseases under control in overcrowded, unnatural conditions. These are the same antibiotics humans use, and that low-level but constant use is the perfect recipe for superbugs to evolve, meaning we are losing these life-saving drugs so we can have cheaper chicken.

It's easier to grasp how what we eat impacts our home planet when we use the concept of Global Commons. These are the shared international resources of polar ice caps, land mass, stable weather, abundant biodiversity, vibrant nutrient cycles, healthy oceans, swathes of forests and flowing fresh water, that together keep our planet, the global economy and ultimately human civilization stable. Disruption to these Global Commons is also what creates threats to that stability, most notably climate change and biodiversity collapse.

Yet the more we relinquish our food to the control of the few with nothing but profit as their ultimate aim, the more we lose. Extensive consolidation of the seed industry in the past 70 years has resulted in the closure of most independent seed merchants. It has also led to the loss of regionally adapted plant varieties that suit local soils and conditions in favour of hybridized varieties typically bred for high yields. The UN Food and Agricultural Organization estimates that the loss of genetic diversity in plants globally stands at 75% along with the disappearance of 93% of our unique seed varieties in the past 100 years. That's fuelling the loss of those treasured special ingredients as farmers produce cash crops instead of local food.

Instead most industrially produced food relies on just nine globally traded crops, such as wheat, maize, sugar and soya. Native breeds, perfectly adapted to all corners of the globe, are being lost in favour of fast-growing hybrids fed on soya instead of grass (more on this on page 99). And crucially, our money lines the pockets of investors and shareholders so they can buy another holiday home, instead of local farmers and community shops who use that money to care for their elderly parents, or take their kids to the football club or a swimming lesson.

When this system of feeding ourselves is examined through a capitalist lens, the market economy appears to do the job; people have plenty of food to eat at the lowest price as dictated by the market economy. Yet as with so many things, it isn't that simple. Having cheap food when there are no local rural jobs, a loss of antibiotics, a destroyed natural environment, biodiversity collapse, and a climate crisis fuelled by reckless carbon release, deforestation and agrochemical pollution, that dinner loses its appeal.

Now with soaring diet-related health issues, the true cost of industrially produced food is surfacing, and with a nation that has lost the ability to cook, leaving us tied to the food system which is doing so much harm to our health, economy, countryside, wildlife and society.

Cookery skills have been handed down the generations for millennia, but in less than a decade just 43% of people cook for their families every day in the UK, while one in eight never cooks from scratch. This means fewer parents are equipped to teach their children how to cook, and so the crisis deepens. Jamie Oliver sums it up brilliantly: 'Every child deserves to learn the basics about food – where it comes from, how to cook it and how it affects their bodies. These life skills are as important as reading and writing.' The erosion of food education in our schools has been well documented, leading to families who are without the skills to lift themselves into nutritious, affordable food. Instead ever shinier marketing campaigns normalize turning to takeaways and convenience food as a means of feeding ourselves.

We need to start thinking about food choices in the same way we now think about plastic use, car journeys and air travel. An instant jump to considering the impact of what we put on our tables. Because when we look at a dish we are looking at a footprint on the earth. We need to think, what food system am I supporting with this purchase? What shape does it push the planet into? It can't change overnight but there is a better path than where we are headed today. An uprising of real farms, real local food, that is connected in a circular economy, with minimal inputs and minimal waste.

Great things can happen when people come together around a table and share good food. It speaks to our history, our humanity, our planet and our future. If that food is produced with reverence and care, this is what lifts the simple act of feeding ourselves to truly stirring stuff.

This is a lovely way to convince even the most sceptical of offal eaters that organ meat really is just as delicious as steak. By cooking the heart like a steak and packing in a whole bunch of punchy flavours like chilli heat, loads of herbs and sweet carrots, there is little to offend and they may not even notice they are eating offal at all!

# Lamb's Heart Flatbreads with Chilli, Herb & Carrot Salad

— SERVES 6 —

3 grass-fed lamb's hearts
1 small bunch of mint,
   freshly chopped
1 small bunch of dill,
   freshly chopped
1 red chilli, deseeded
   and finely chopped
200g (7oz) yogurt
pure sea salt and freshly
   ground black pepper

*For the flatbreads*
300g (10 ½oz) stoneground
   unbleached white flour,
   plus extra for dusting
1 tablespoon olive oil
½ teaspoon fine salt
180ml (6fl oz) warm water

*For the carrot salad*
4 large carrots, scrubbed
   and peeled into thin strips
olive oil
juice of 1 lemon
1 small bunch of mint,
   leaves freshly chopped
1 small bunch of flat-leaf
   parsley, freshly chopped

To make the flatbreads, sift the flour into a bowl. Add the oil, salt and water and bring it together into a dough. Turn it out on to a work surface and knead for 5 minutes until smooth and elastic. If it is too wet and sticky, dust with a bit more flour as you knead it until it behaves. Divide it into 6 equal pieces and form them into balls. Leave them to rest for 5 minutes.

Heat a large, heavy-based frying pan over a high heat. Dust a work surface and a rolling pin with flour. Squash the dough balls into fat discs in your palm, then roll them out as thinly as you can into rough circles. Place the flatbreads in the pan one at time, cooking for about 30 seconds on each side until golden bubbles and blisters form on the surface. Wrap in a tea towel and leave somewhere warm.

To make the salad, dress the carrots with a drizzle of olive oil, salt and pepper, the lemon juice and herbs and set aside.

Prepare the lamb hearts by slicing them into quarters and removing the white sinew with a sharp knife, then season them with a good pinch of salt and pepper.

Preheat a griddle pan until scorchingly hot. Drizzle the hearts with oil and place them into the pan. Cook for 2–3 minutes on each side to get plenty of colour on the hearts, but be careful to avoid overcooking. Remove the hearts from the pan and leave to rest for 5 minutes.

Finely slice the hearts and place on the flatbreads alongside the carrot salad, a scattering of the herbs and chilli and a drizzle of the yogurt. Season to taste.

Sometimes the simplest ways to cook give us the most pleasure. There is nothing complicated about this recipe, a few well-chosen ingredients are made magnificent by the lick of a flame. The herby, aromatic kebabs have a natural affinity with the smoky, charry flavours from cooking over fire.

# Chicken Kebabs with Lime, Lemongrass, Coriander, Yogurt, Basil & Mint

— SERVES 6–8 —

1 free-range chicken, weighing about 1.2–1.5kg (2lb 10oz–3lb 5oz)

2 lemongrass sticks, trimmed and very thinly sliced

4 garlic cloves, grated

½ finger-sized piece of ginger, peeled and grated

zest of 2 limes

6 tablespoons yogurt

1 medium bunch of coriander, stalks and leaves freshly chopped

1 small bunch of mint, leaves freshly chopped

1 small bunch of basil, leaves freshly chopped

2 teaspoons cumin seeds, crushed

2 teaspoons coriander seeds, crushed

2 tablespoons olive oil

pure sea salt and freshly ground black pepper

6–8 wooden barbecue skewers (soaked in water to stop them burning)

Place the chicken on a board and remove the breasts and legs (you can follow our guide to How to Butcher A Bird on page 82). Skin and cube the breast meat into 3–4cm (1¼–1½in) chunks. Remove the meat from the legs and thighs and cut into similar-sized pieces. Save the carcass for making stock (see page 21).

Pop the chicken meat in a bowl and add all the other ingredients, except the oil and seasoning. Turn everything together so the chicken gets really well-coated in the yogurt. Cover and leave to marinate for 3–6 hours or overnight.

To assemble the kebabs, thread the herby chicken pieces on to wooden skewers or kebab sticks (making sure you get as much fragrant herby yogurt as you can on there too) – 6–8 pieces should make a good-sized kebab. Once you've threaded them all up, season them generously with salt and pepper.

Prepare your fire. You want hot embers, but not ragingly hot, or the kebabs will cook too quickly. When the fire is ready, set a grill over the top, trickle the kebabs with a little olive oil and lay them down over it. Cook for 6–8 minutes on each side, keeping a close eye on them, so as not to let them burn. Leave the kebabs to rest somewhere warm for 5 minutes before serving with flatbreads (see page 108), a fresh tomato salad and pickled green chillies.

Panzanella salad was perfected by ever-resourceful Tuscan farmers. It uses ingredients that are grown in abundance in the Tuscan countryside, that ripen quickly, creating a glut and, with a frugality that is often commonplace in farming communities, makes use of stale bread. An important detail of this dish is you must give it a little time to sit before serving – this is the step that is most difficult to do considering you will want to dive right in immediately, but time is really where the magic happens.

# Panzanella Salad with Fire-cooked Chicken Thighs

— SERVES 4 —

extra virgin olive oil
4 free-range chicken thighs, skin on
leftover sourdough bread
2 punnets of cherry tomatoes, sliced
1 large red onion, thinly sliced
1 bunch of basil, leaves torn
3 teaspoons balsamic vinegar
pure sea salt

Fill the bottom of your barbecue with sustainable lumpwood charcoal. Using one or two natural firelighters, light the coals and allow them to heat up and develop a grey coat.

Take a heavy cast-iron frying pan and place over the heat of the barbecue. While the pan heats up, generously season the thighs with oil and salt. Place the chicken thighs skin-side down in the pan and cook for about 4 minutes. Turn the thighs over and cook on the other side for a further 4 minutes until they are golden and crispy.

Take the leftover sourdough and slice it into cubes. Add the sourdough to the pan and continue to fry the thighs and sourdough until everything is crispy and golden. Remove the chicken thighs from the pan and leave to rest.

Roughly chop the chicken thighs into 4 pieces and add to a mixing bowl. To the bowl, add the crispy sourdough cubes, tomatoes, red onion slices, basil leaves, balsamic vinegar, a good drizzle of olive oil and a generous pinch of salt and mix together.

Leave to sit for 10–15 minutes before serving to allow all the ingredients time to get to know each other.

For us, wings make the perfect fodder for larger gatherings, when the greedy crowd descends and you need to satiate them quickly. They can be made ahead of time and cooked quickly, leaving you time to focus on other more complex outdoor cookery, or simply to enjoy a glass of wine in the sunshine with your guests.

# Black Garlic Glazed Chicken Wings

— SERVES 4 —

1kg (2lb 4oz) chicken wings
olive oil
1 teaspoon sesame seeds, toasted
1 small bunch of coriander, leaves picked
pure sea salt and freshly ground black pepper
lime wedges, to serve

*For the black garlic glaze*
2 tablespoons water
6 black garlic cloves, finely chopped
2 tablespoons balsamic vinegar
2 tablespoons honey
2 tablespoons dark soy sauce

Preheat the oven to 160°C/325°F/gas mark 3.

Drizzle the chicken wings with a little olive oil and season well with salt and pepper. Place on a wide baking tray and gently roast in the oven for 30 minutes.

Meanwhile, prepare the black garlic glaze. Place the water, black garlic, balsamic vinegar, honey and soy sauce in a small saucepan and simmer gently for a few minutes to form a glaze.

Remove the chicken wings from the oven and drain any fat that has rendered out of the wings as that will prevent the glaze from sticking.

Increase the oven temperature to 200°C/400°F/gas mark 6.

Pour the glaze over the chicken and return to the oven for 10 minutes, then turn the wings to ensure they cook evenly and return to the oven for a further 10 minutes, or until nicely glazed and golden.

Place the chicken on a platter, scatter with the sesame seeds and coriander and serve with the lime wedges.

This recipe is a testament that you don't need a whole host of complicated ingredients to make a special meal, just a few handfuls of summer-glut veg, paired with a seriously good steak. As the tomatoes blister and cook down they create an incredible sauce that can be spooned over the steak, mixing with the meaty juices. Pure magic.

# Fire-cooked Sirloin Steaks with Spicy Tomatoes & Runner Beans

— SERVES 2 —

2 grass-fed beef sirloin steaks
olive oil
1 tablespoon grass-fed butter
½ red onion, sliced
1 sprig of thyme
a large handful of
    cherry tomatoes
1 bunch of runner beans,
    chopped
1 red chilli, chopped
1 garlic clove, chopped
1 small bunch of basil,
    freshly chopped
pure sea salt

In the base of your barbecue, pour in about a quarter of a standard bag of sustainable lumpwood charcoal. Set alight and wait until the coals have developed a thick grey coat.

Generously season the sirloin steaks with some salt and a drizzle of oil. Take a heavy-based frying pan and place over the heat of the fire, allowing it to get smoking hot. Place the steaks in the pan and caramelize for a few minutes on each side. You want to cook the steaks for no more than 7 minutes.

Add the butter, onion, thyme and the cherry tomatoes to the pan and flip around the pan, allowing all of the flavours to mingle. Remove the steaks from the pan and leave to rest.

Continue to cook the cherry tomatoes until they start to break down and soften. At this stage, add the beans, chilli and garlic. Gently stew the beans in the soft tomatoes for a few minutes until they soften slightly, not too much though as you want them to retain a little bite.

Serve the steaks alongside the glorious veggies. Finish with a pinch of salt and some chopped basil.

In this recipe, roast figs burst in the hot oven and combine their wonderfully sweet juices with rich, fatty pork chops paired with aromatic fennel and minerally cavolo nero. The flavours in this dish are evocative of the balmy Mediterranean in late summer.

# Pork Chops, Roast Figs, Fennel & Cavolo Nero

— SERVES 2 —

2 small fennel heads, each cut into 4, lengthways
1 garlic clove, chopped
2 teaspoons fennel seeds
olive oil
6 figs, halved
1 large rosemary sprig
5 bay leaves
175ml (6fl oz) red wine
1 litre (1¾ pints) chicken stock (see page 21)
a handful of cavolo nero or kale, roughly sliced
40g (1½oz) unsalted grass-fed butter
2 native breed pork chops
drizzle olive oil
pure sea salt and freshly ground black pepper

Preheat the oven to 200°C/400°F/gas mark 6.

Place the fennel in a roasting tray with the garlic, sprinkle with fennel seeds, drizzle with olive oil and season with a good pinch of salt. Place in the oven and roast for 10 minutes.

Remove the fennel from the oven and add the figs, rosemary and bay leaves, then roast for another 10 minutes until the figs start to leak their juices. Remove the tray from the oven and pour in the wine.

Place the tray on the hob and reduce the wine down to a glaze. Now pour in the stock and reduce slowly for 10 minutes or so before adding the cavolo nero. Cook for a further 5 minutes until the sauce is nicely reduced and the cavolo nero is tender. Stir in the butter and season with salt and pepper.

Place a large frying pan over high heat. Season the pork chops, rub with a little oil and then sear them for 3–4 minutes on each side or until nicely browned.

Using tongs, stand them up on the fatty side and sear them for a minute to help caramelize and render the fat. Transfer to the oven and finish cooking for a further 6 minutes. Remove the pork chops from the oven and leave to rest somewhere warm for 5 minutes. Pour the pork resting juices into the veg.

Divide the fennel, figs and sauce between 2 plates and serve with the chops.

# September

Summer seems to last forever until all at once it collapses into autumn with an exhausted sigh. The golden autumnal light pours over the backs of our Red Ruby cattle that contentedly graze the pasture. Meanwhile, the ewes are brought down from their summer grazing on higher ground for health checks before we put them to the ram.

As the evenings draw in, dusk is filled with bats flittering around the barns. Hedgerows are loaded with swollen berries and an old wax jacket is required to fight the barbs and spikes and win armfuls of sloes and blackberries for the larder.

There is nothing better than a hearty Sunday roast after a long walk, crunching through the leaves on a golden, autumnal day. Pork belly is a beautifully hearty and indulgent cut of meat with a rich flavour, that will leave everyone fighting over the salty crackling on the top. One of the joys of slowly reared native breed pork is that there is always plenty of unctuous fat. Nothing beats rich, buttery, sweet pork fat once it has been gently rendered into submission during a long, slow cook. In this recipe the apples soften down and release a delicious sweetness which harmonizes perfectly with the salty tang from the pork, providing a unique twist on a classic roast dinner.

# Roast Pork Belly with Baked Apples

— SERVES 8 —

1.5kg (3lb 5oz) pork
  belly, scored
1 red onion, cut into wedges
8 rashers of unsmoked bacon
8 small apples, such as Cox's
1 small bunch of sage,
  leaves picked
8 bay leaves
a handful of fennel fronds
  (optional)
2 teaspoons fennel seeds,
  crushed
2 tablespoons olive oil
pure sea salt and freshly
  ground black pepper

Preheat the oven to 230°C/450°F/gas mark 8.

Place the pork (with its very dry skin – this is really important as we want it to crackle) in a suitably sized roasting tin. Season all over with salt, then place in the oven for 25–30 minutes. Once the crackling is looking good, remove the pork and reduce the oven temperature to 190°C/375°F/gas mark 5.

Scatter the red onion wedges over the base of a large, ovenproof dish. Carefully lift the pork from the hot roasting tin and set it down on top of the onions.

Wind a piece of bacon around the circumference of each apple and hold it in place with a toothpick. Place the apples around the pork, scatter over the sage leaves, bay and fennel fronds (if using) and season well with salt and pepper. Sprinkle over the crushed fennel seeds and trickle everything with the olive oil.

Transfer the dish to the oven and cook for 35 minutes until the pork is cooked through and the apples are soft but not collapsing. (It's worth noting that if the apples look like they are going to collapse, you can take them out of the oven and allow the pork to finish cooking without them.)

Remove the dish from the oven and leave the meat to rest in a warm place for 10–15 minutes. Serve everyone a few thick slices of pork, some generous strips of crackling, an apple and some herby juices.

Proper mixed farming requires rotational cropping, a common-sense practice that allows nature to perform its magic in circular fashion, recycling and reusing energy from one enterprise as it finishes, to the other as it begins. There is an old adage, 'what grows together goes together', and this couldn't be more true when it comes to squash and pork. Squash loves rich, fertile soil and thrives buried deep in a submerged city of bugs and worms. The nutrients are sucked up by the plants' roots to create vegetables that keep wonderfully throughout the autumn and winter.

# Sausage & Squash Gnocchi
## — SERVES 4 —

*For the gnocchi*
1 medium squash, such as
    Crown Prince, deseeded
    and quartered
olive oil
3 tablespoons stoneground
    unbleached white flour
½ teaspoon grated nutmeg
1 free-range and/or organic egg
    yolk, beaten (optional)
semolina, for dusting
pure sea salt and freshly
    ground black pepper

*For the sausages*
olive oil
6 sausages, cooked and
    sliced into 1cm (½in) slices
1 tablespoon salted
    grass-fed butter
2 garlic cloves, finely sliced
1 small bunch of thyme,
    finely chopped
3 sprigs of sage, leaves picked
250ml (9fl oz) white wine
200ml (7fl oz) single cream
1 small bunch of flat-leaf
    parsley, finely chopped
hard cheese, such as Old
    Winchester, or clothbound
    goat's cheese, such as
    Quicke's (optional)

Preheat the oven to 200°C/400°F/gas mark 6.

Dress the squash with olive oil and season well with salt and pepper. Roast in a small baking tray for 30 minutes or until tender. Leave to cool a little, then scoop the squash out of its skin and mash the flesh into a fairly smooth purée. Add the purée to a medium saucepan and cook over a low heat for about 15 minutes, keeping the squash moving so it doesn't stick. This will help to dry out the squash. Place the purée in a bowl and leave to cool to room temperature.

Add the flour and nutmeg to the squash purée, plus any additional salt and pepper required. Combine together to form a dough. The dough should be soft but workable. If it feels too wet, add a little more flour. If it feels too dry, carefully add a beaten egg yolk.

Dust a work surface with semolina. Roll out portions of the dough into long cylinders and cut into roughly 4cm (1½in) gnocchi. Place on a tray heavily dusted with semolina to prevent them from sticking.

Place a wide, heavy-based frying pan over a medium–high heat. Add a drizzle of olive oil along with the sausages. Add the butter, garlic, thyme and sage leaves and sizzle for a few minutes. Add the white wine and reduce until it has nearly disappeared, then add the cream and reduce the liquor by about a third.

Bring a large pan of salted water to a rolling boil. Add the gnocchi and cook for 2–3 minutes; they are ready when they float to the surface. Use a slotted spoon to remove the gnocchi and add them to the pan with the sausage mixture. Toss the pan to combine everything.

Finish with the parsley and a grating of hard cheese, if you like.

If you're looking for a 'hearty' breakfast (we just couldn't resist!) look no further than this classic. Sweetness, spice, cream and alcohol, all the good things are covered in this grown-up feast. Generously slosh over thick, buttered sourdough toast and serve with mugs of tea for a proper farmhouse breakfast.

# Devilled Hearts on Toast

— SERVES 2 —

250g (9oz) free-range
    chicken hearts
olive oil
125ml (4fl oz) cider brandy
    (we like Somerset Cider
    Brandy Co Kingston Black
    Apple Aperitif)
1½ teaspoons cider vinegar
1 teaspoon Worcestershire sauce
1 teaspoon Dijon mustard
pinch of cayenne pepper
1 teaspoon redcurrant jelly
2–3 tablespoons double cream
2 large slices of sourdough
    bread, toasted and buttered
1 small bunch of flat-leaf
    parsley, finely chopped
pure sea salt and freshly
    ground black pepper

Prepare the chicken hearts by slicing them in half and trimming away any larger bits of sinew.

Heat a large, heavy-based frying pan over a medium–high heat. Add a drizzle of oil and the chicken hearts and fry hard for 1–2 minutes, no more; the hearts should take on a little colour. Remove from the pan and set aside.

To the pan, add the cider brandy and reduce to a syrup. Then add the cider vinegar, Worcestershire sauce, Dijon mustard, cayenne pepper and redcurrant jelly. Combine and bring the pan to a gentle bubble. Add the double cream and reduce the liquor by a quarter. Check the seasoning and add salt and pepper, to taste. Add the chicken hearts back to the pan and mix through the glorious sauce.

Dollop the devilled hearts on top of the buttered toast and finish with some chopped flat-leaf parsley.

Mutton loin is an exquisite cut and it's got an incredible depth of flavour but it's also one of the tenderest parts of the animal. This recipe is packed full of interesting textures and exciting flavours and makes a little mutton go a long way.

# Roast Mutton Loin with Spiced Carrots, Flatbreads & Tahini Yogurt

— SERVES 4 —

500g (1lb 2oz) grass-fed
  mutton loin
a few sprigs of rosemary
a few sprigs of thyme
flatbreads (see page 108)
pure sea salt and freshly
  ground black pepper

*For the tahini yogurt*
1 tablespoon tahini
3–4 tablespoons yogurt
1 tablespoon extra virgin
  olive oil
juice of 1 lemon
½ small garlic clove, grated
a pinch of pure sea salt

*For the roast carrots*
12 medium bunched carrots,
  trimmed, scrubbed and
  halved lengthways
1 medium onion, thinly sliced
4 garlic cloves, thinly sliced
3 teaspoons coriander seeds,
  lightly crushed
3 teaspoons fennel seeds,
  lightly crushed
2 pinches of ancho chilli flakes,
  plus extra to serve
2 sprigs of rosemary
3–4 sprigs of thyme
3 tablespoons extra virgin olive
  oil, plus extra to serve
2 tablespoons toasted pumpkin
  seeds (optional)

Preheat the oven to 180°C/350°F/gas mark 4.

Combine all the ingredients for the tahini yogurt together in a bowl and mix well. If it's too thick, add a dash of cold water to thin it a little. Set aside.

Place the carrots in a medium–large roasting tray with the sliced onion, garlic, crushed spice seeds and chilli flakes. Tear over the herbs and trickle with the olive oil. Season with salt and pepper, then tumble together. Place the tray in the oven and roast for 45–50 minutes, stirring regularly, until the carrots are tender.

Meanwhile, place the mutton loin in a pan or small roasting tray with the herbs and season all over with salt and pepper. Roast for 25–30 minutes or until the centre of the meat has reached 55–60°C (131–140°F) on a digital temperature probe. When the mutton and carrots are cooked, remove them from the oven and leave to rest somewhere warm.

To serve, pile some carrots on to each flatbread. Slice the mutton and arrange this over the carrots. Spoon over some tahini yogurt and finish with a pinch of chilli flakes and some toasted pumpkin seeds if you like.

Let's be honest, scrag end isn't the sexiest name. If you can see past this rather crude moniker, you will be rewarded with all sorts of unctuous goodness. Rich fat, collagen and marrow are aplenty in this cut, all melting together to form a sumptuous sauce with little bites of deliciously flaky meat. Serve smothered over fresh tagliatelle.

# Braised Scrag End of Mutton with Tomatoes & Tagliatelle

— SERVES 4 —

olive oil
600g (1lb 5oz) scrag
    end of mutton
1 onion, chopped
4 garlic cloves, chopped
2 bay leaves
2 sprigs of rosemary,
    leaves freshly chopped
250ml (9fl oz) red wine
680g (1lb 8oz) jar passata
400g (14oz) fresh tagliatelle
a handful of flat-leaf parsley,
    freshly chopped
hard goat's cheese (we like
    Quicke's), grated (optional)
pure sea salt and freshly
    ground black pepper

Preheat the oven to 150°C/300°F/gas mark 2.

Take an ovenproof dish and place it over a high heat. Drizzle a little olive oil in the dish, season the mutton, then place it into the dish and caramelize the mutton for about 5 minutes on each side, or until golden brown. Remove the meat from the pan and set it aside.

Add the onion, garlic, bay leaves and rosemary to the dish. Sweat the onion down for about 5 minutes and allow the herbs to infuse their woody aromatics. Add the red wine and passata, then bring to the boil.

Return the mutton to the dish, place the lid on top and gently cook in the oven for 3 hours, or until the meat is tender and falling off the bone. You may need to top up the dish with a little water to stop it from drying out.

Place a pan of salted water over a high heat and bring to the boil. Add the tagliatelle and cook for about 5 minutes. Drain the pasta, reserving a cup of the salted cooking water.

Remove the mutton from the oven and place it on the hob over a medium heat. Add the salted water to the tomato sauce and simmer. Remove the bones from the sauce and check the seasoning. Remove the dish from the heat. Add the pasta to the dish and cover generously with the flaky meat and tomato sauce.

Serve with a little chopped flat-leaf parsley over the top and, if you're feeling really indulgent, a few grates of hard goat's cheese.

# Native Breeds & Why They Matter

———

On the wild coasts of Exmoor there's a memorable sight to be seen in winter. Cattle with a rich, tufty, auburn coat curled into licks, peer out from faces caked in salt crystals. These are Ruby Red Devons, a hardy native breed that forages in the moorland landscape, feeding on rough grasses that few modern livestock breeds would contemplate. On these hills where the moors meet the cliffs, the winter weather blasts salt-laden air inland, coating the vegetation and the cattle in fine white sea salt. It's brutal at times, but these are animals that have thrived in this landscape for centuries, bred to have thick protective coats, to be nurturing mothers and to produce delicious meat off meagre grazing thanks to an admirable hardiness.

Red Rubies (as they are known in farming circles) are one of many native livestock breeds that collectively offer a treasure trove of environmental and culinary riches. For centuries farmers and smallholders developed lineages of livestock from goats to cattle, sheep to pigs, beautifully adapted to the different regional climates and rural habitats across the British Isles, as have communities all over the world. Careful cross-breeding was used to favour desirable features such as milk productivity in dairy cows, meat marbling in beef cattle, mothering instincts in pigs and lambing frequency in ewes.

Crucially, this would all be in the context of these animals eating nothing but the food that was already plentiful where they were. For cattle and sheep this could be moorland grazing in the uplands, or pastures, meadows and coastal salt marshes at lower altitudes, while for pigs it would be rooting in woodlands for beech mast and acorns and in turnip fields, or on kitchen scraps from the farmhouse. All of them would

effortlessly convert modest natural food into meat, milk and useful by-products such as leather, fleeces and fat. Grass would be supplemented as needed in the winter with stored alternatives – hay, silage and fodder, such as beets or traditional arable crops like barley which needed little to flourish in the British climate. Fertility to boost crop or pasture growth came from the livestock itself in a balanced cycle that required little to no input from beyond the farm gate.

Today the mainstream meat and dairy system is very different. Hybridized breeds are the focus, animals whose genome may be patented and owned by agricultural tech giants. These sprinters produce significantly more meat or milk per animal as they are typically larger, leaner and faster-growing than traditional breeds, creating the economies of scale and favourable reduced 'unit cost' for the industrialized system. Simply put, there is more milk per animal or more meat per carcass hook, faster. As with most perceived advantages however, this comes at a price. With thin skins and a huge hunger to feed all that growth and productivity, they need an athlete's diet to match and have a constitution that puts them at the more fragile end of the spectrum compared to those hardy native breeds.

This is where what we feed our livestock becomes an important issue. Grains such as barley, wheat and maize are more nutrient-dense than grass alone and have been used to supplement cattle feed for decades, particularly to speed up the 'finishing' phase of getting an animal to slaughter weight. Some hybrid dairy cattle don't have the ability to eat, digest and process a natural grass diet fast enough to fuel the production of milk their bodies have been bred to produce. In the 1940s and 50s complete 'concentrate' feeds were developed, designed to give livestock all the nutrition they needed in every bite. This comes in the form of pellets called nuts or rolls, formulated by nutritionists from commodity-traded grains, and making use of manufacturing by-products such as spent cooking oils or processing pomaces, and was a convenient way for the farmer to know that the animals had everything they needed from their diet. More recently soya has also been piled into these, as its high protein content is particularly easy for animals to digest, making that growth all the swifter. The numbers are staggering: 27 million tonnes of soya was grown in 1961, and in 2018 that figure stood at 350 million – 70% of it was fed to livestock.

*Our native breeds were animals bred to thrive on a simple, natural diet that required no flown-in, globally traded, manufactured feed with a huge environmental impact.*

It's a similar story with all the classic British farm animals; native breeds have been pushed to the margins to make way for hybrids with high productivity of meat or milk that the industrial system favours. Where once farms across the country had their distinct local breeds which were venerated and treasured, now the vast majority of livestock from intensive systems are from just a few commercial variants, fed on manufactured feed blends based on globally traded ingredients. In contrast those native breeds were animals bred to thrive on a simple diet that required no flown-in, globally traded, manufactured feed.

These global food economics distort local systems. Vast monocultures across the world produce arable crops to feed livestock. Forced to move to economies of scale with fast-growing breeds, with calculated daily rations of feed, farmers move animals indoors and rural jobs are reduced. Food produced locally is sold globally, has to be transported to distant processing plants and packhouses, rather than being consumed where it is grown and reared, with a far smaller footprint.

The loss is cultural too. The poetic names of native breeds at risk of disappearing are loaded with meaning and history: Lincoln Longwool and Whitefaced Dartmoor sheep, White Park and Vaynol cattle, British Lop and Tamworth pigs, Brecon Buff geese, Harvey Speckled turkeys and Shetland ducks. When carefully managed, native breeds are a powerful conservation tool as well, happily grazing uneven, hilly land that is unsuitable for growing crops, and boosting biodiversity as they move through the landscape, clearing spaces for other species and encouraging insect life with their dung and the trophic cascade that follows.

Grass-fed native livestock breeds grow slowly. This allows the flavour of the meat to develop, for the marrow, cartilage and marbling to be loaded with nutrients, meaning each cut goes further as you only need a little to impart a meaty, satisfying element to the dish. Vegetables cooked in beef dripping, or rice cooked in lamb stock give you the umami hit without the heft of industrial meat's dizzying environmental impact.

The demand for meat, and cheap meat at that, is at the heart of the issue. Global meat production has tripled in the last 50 years, powered by all this breeding and feed innovation. It is unrealistic to think that we can go back to a time when meat was farmed in balance with the countryside at the rate it is consumed today. What we can do is eat far less of it, and question where it comes from, what it eats and where it roamed. Less and better is the way forward. We need to reclaim our food system at the farm gate. That's where hope lives.

It's easy to get stuck in a rut with your cooking, particularly when that rut is absolutely delicious. Take roast chicken for example; sometimes it's hard to see why you'd do anything else with a good bird, when it's so simple and so tasty. However, from time to time it's always worth changing things up and, when you do, this is the perfect dish to make.

# Chicken with Olives, Preserved Lemons & Herbs

## — SERVES 6 —

1 free-range chicken
1 tablsepoon olive oil
100g (3½oz) chorizo
2 red peppers, cut into 1cm- (½in-)thick lengths
1 large onion, thinly sliced
2 garlic cloves, thinly sliced
2 teaspoons fennel seeds
1 tablespoon tomato purée
½ tablespoon smoked paprika
150g (5½oz) pearled spelt or barley, soaked in fresh water for 1 hour and drained
a pinch of saffron (optional)
100g (3½oz) pitted green olives
3–4 sprigs of marjoram
500ml (18fl oz) chicken stock (see page 21)
1 preserved lemon
6 fresh bay leaves
pure sea salt and freshly ground black pepper
1 small bunch of flat-leaf parsley, leaves picked and chopped, to garnish

Preheat the oven to 180°C/350°F/gas mark 4.

Place the chicken on a large chopping board. Use a sharp knife to remove the legs and the wings. Cut the breasts away from the bird and halve them. (Follow our guide to How to Butcher a Bird on page 82.)

Set a large, heavy-based casserole dish over a medium heat. Add the olive oil and when it's hot, add the chicken pieces. Season them with salt and pepper and fry them, turning regularly until they are crisping, golden and smelling delicious. Lift the chicken out to a plate.

Slice the chorizo into chunky rounds and add it to the pan, along with the red peppers, onion, garlic, fennel seeds, tomato purée and paprika. Fry, stirring regularly, for 8–10 minutes.

Now add the pearled spelt, saffron (if using), green olives, marjoram and chicken stock. Give it all a stir, then arrange the chicken pieces over the top of the spelt and peppers. Cut the preserved lemon into quarters, discard the flesh and thinly slice the skin. Scatter this around the chicken. Tuck in the bay leaves and place a lid on the pan. Cook in the oven for 1 hour.

The chicken should be nice and tender and the meat coming away from the bone with ease.

Leave to rest for 15 minutes, then garnish with the parsley and serve with crusty bread.

As the weather starts to become unsettled and we spend more time sheltering under trees, there is a dish that our hearts call out for. Something simple to put together, which provides comfort and nourishment; our family's version of the classic 'Swedish Meatballs'. The Scandinavians are famously happy people, and with dishes like this one at the heart of the homestead, it's not difficult to see why.

# Swedish Meatballs

— SERVES 2 —

1 tablespoon unsalted
　grass-fed butter
1 onion, finely diced
400g (14oz) Saddleback
　pork mince
100g (3½oz) fresh breadcrumbs
1 small bunch of dill, finely
　chopped, plus extra to serve
1 large free-range and/or
　organic egg, beaten
1 tablespoon olive oil
2 tablespoons stoneground
　unbleached white flour
400ml (14fl oz) hot beef stock
　(see page 22)
100ml (3½fl oz) double cream
pure sea salt and freshly
　ground black pepper

Preheat the oven to 180°C/350°F/gas mark 4.

Take a cast-iron pan and place over a medium heat. Add a little of the butter and the diced onion to the pan and sweat the onion down for 5–6 minutes until just starting to turn translucent.

In a mixing bowl, place the pork mince, breadcrumbs, dill, onions and egg, season generously and combine the ingredients. Once evenly mixed, shape the mixture into meatballs about 2.5cm (1in) each.

In the pan you used to cook off your onions, add the oil and bring to a medium–high heat. Fry the meatballs for 3–4 minutes on each side until they are gloriously golden. Remove them from the pan, place on to a baking sheet and put into the warm oven while you make the sauce.

Take the pan that you cooked the meatballs in (it should be full of delicious pork fat and crispy bits of pork), place over a medium heat and add the remaining butter. Add the flour and stir it into the butter to make a roux. Cook the roux for a few minutes until sandy in texture and then gradually whisk in the hot stock and cook, stirring all the time, until the sauce simmers and thickens.

Remove the meatballs from the oven and add to the pan, then stir in the double cream. Check the seasoning and finish the dish, as the Scandinavians do, with some chopped dill sprinkled over the top. Serve with buttery mash.

# October

Rain pitter-patters against the window as the kettle sings, calling us to make another cup of tea and shelter for a minute longer in the embrace of the kitchen. Mud rises up our boots like the markings of the tide on the shoreline, and ugly waterproof trousers are our best friend. The pasture is being tested – and like a dutiful sponge it does its very best to soak away and recycle the abundance of rainwater.

Pastures are peppered with field mushrooms, puffballs and horse mushrooms ripe for picking. As if blown away by the rising winds, the last few swallows disappear from sight, leaving their carefully constructed nests bare until they return.

There are few things in life more welcoming than the scent of a roast chicken – it has to be the ultimate comfort food, the sort of dish that brings people together around the kitchen table. This recipe for pot-roast chicken is good-mood food, and good-mood cooking, too. You just throw everything in the pot and let it roast away merrily. A wonderfully simple way to honour a whole bird.

# Pot-roast Chicken with Fennel & Cider Broth

— SERVES 4 —

1.5kg (3lb 5oz) free-range
    chicken
olive oil
2 fennel bulbs, quartered
4 shallots, halved
4 garlic cloves, bashed
a small handful of bay leaves
a small handful of sage leaves
2 sprigs of rosemary
400ml (14fl oz) dry cider
500ml (18fl oz) chicken stock
    (see page 21)
pure sea salt and freshly
    ground black pepper

Preheat the oven to 180°C/350°F/gas mark 4.

Take a solid, lidded casserole dish and place it over a high heat. Generously oil and season the chicken with salt and pepper, making sure you also season the inside of the cavity. Place into the smoking hot casserole dish and carefully fry the chicken, moving it around in the dish with a pair of tongs. You want to get the outside of the skin lovely and brown – this will take 7–8 minutes.

To the casserole dish, add the fennel, shallots, garlic and herbs. Roast in the oven for 15 minutes.

Remove the casserole dish from the oven and add the cider and chicken stock, put the lid on and return to the oven for a further 45 minutes.

Remove the dish from the oven and carefully remove the whole chicken using a pair of tongs. Leave the bird to rest for 10 minutes. Taste the chicken and cider broth and adjust the seasoning as required.

Carve the chicken and serve with the braised fennel and broth. Enjoy with homemade aioli (see page 116) and a slice of sourdough bread.

This is what we call real comfort food. A lump of our slowly reared native breed pork accompanied by a luscious creamy gratin, this dish really is heaven in a bowl and the perfect thing for slow Sundays. Roasting the pastured pork on top of the woody herbs in this way infuses the meat with subtle aromatics that bring the eating experience to a new place entirely. Don't skimp on the milk – seek out that wonderful old-fashioned cream-topped milk to truly take this recipe to new heights.

# Roast Pork with Creamy Fennel & Leek Gratin

— SERVES 6 —

1 sprig of thyme
1 sprig of rosemary
1 sprig of sage
1kg (2lb 4oz) Saddleback pork leg

*For the gratin*
250ml (9fl oz) whole Jersey milk from grass-fed cows
500ml (18fl oz) double cream
2 bay leaves
100g (3½oz) dried wild or porcini mushrooms
2 garlic cloves, chopped
3 fennel bulbs
2 leeks
150g (5½oz) clothbound Cheddar cheese
pure sea salt and freshly ground black pepper

Preheat the oven to 200°C/400°F/gas mark 6.

Fill the bottom of a roasting dish with garden herbs – we like the woody aromatics of thyme, rosemary and sage – then place the pork leg on top of the herbs and cover the skin generously with salt.

Roast in the oven for 30 minutes to allow the skin to crisp and crackle, then reduce the temperature to 180°C/350°F/gas mark 4 and roast for a further 30–35 minutes, or until the core temperature of the joint reaches 50°C (122°F) using a digital temperature probe. Remove from the oven and leave to rest somewhere warm for 20 minutes.

To make the gratin, pour the milk and the cream into a pan, then add the bay leaves, mushrooms and garlic. Gently warm through to allow all of the aromatics to take hold of the liquid. Bring to a simmer, then remove from the heat and leave to infuse for a further 20 minutes. Generously season the cream, so that the liquor can season your other ingredients.

Finely shred the fennel and the leeks, then pack tightly into a shallow baking dish. Pour the infused cream over the top of the vegetables and grate the Cheddar over the top. Bake in the oven for 35 minutes until the cheese is gloriously golden.

Carve the roasted pork leg into thick slices with a generous helping of crackling. Serve with a heap of the rich gratin alongside for a true taste of autumn.

# The Culinary & Environmental Glory of Venison

———

Take a morning walk on a country lane and, with a little lingering and observation, chances are the land will tell you stories of creatures you don't see. The secret life of the countryside laid out in track prints, wildlife paths and snuffle holes. Mud is especially helpful, often rewarding the walker with track prints of foraging birds, skittering mice, fleeting rabbits, travelling badgers and more often than not, deer. Thousands of these elusive creatures cruise through our woods, fields and valleys, and they are an untapped, low-impact food resource that can help reduce the environmental impact of our diets to a surprising degree.

There are six species that roam the UK to varying degrees: the native red and roe deer alongside the introduced species of fallow, sika, muntjac and Chinese water deer. Indeed, there are over 30 species in the whole of Europe with similarly buoyant populations. These animals typically prefer a mixed environment of woodland and open fields, so the British countryside creates the perfect place, with farmland, parks and even suburban gardens all playing host to this shy, flighty mammal.

Historically their populations would have been kept under control by lynx and wolves, which would also have moved the animals on constantly, preventing any extensive damage to a particular area. It is estimated that there are now over two million deer in the UK, the highest number for 1,000 years. Unfortunately, as the population has exploded and breakaway herds and ousted individuals seek new territories, they are increasingly causing accidents on roads, many of a serious nature.

There was a time when the story of deer in this country was very different. By the eighteenth century red and roe deer were so prized for their meat and as an accessible wild food for poorer communities that they were almost driven to extinction. Protection measures were put in place and over the years venison drifted off our kitchen tables for all but the most privileged. More recently, as the supermarket systems and industrially produced meat exiled anything that didn't fit into the always-there supply chain, venison faded into obscurity. A loss of cooking skills has compounded the issue, alongside concern over gamey flavours and the distorted view of venison as meat for the wealthy (it was a favourite of King Henry VIII), or special occasions only.

Yet those excessive populations are becoming an ever bigger problem. The deer's predilection for juicy young plants and tree bark has an impact on biodiversity too, preventing regeneration of woodlands, impacting tree planting and rewilding enterprises and selectively eating plant species to the extent that they out-compete other wildlife. It depends on context of course; deer essentially engineer woodland areas through physically trampling and wallowing, which can create better biodiversity up to a point, but overpopulation ultimately leads to habitat degradation. In short, they've become a secret pest at these levels.

In the absence of apex predators, deer numbers are managed through culling, but much of the meat ends up at two very different ends of the spectrum: pet food or fine dining restaurants. Yet venison is an abundant, delicious meat that is there for everyone. The source just needs a little scrutiny, and the cooking a little consideration, but it deserves a place on the considered carnivore's table.

So how exactly does venison end up in our food chain? There are three main routes: wild, farmed or parkland deer. Farmed deer are produced in the least natural, most

intensive system. At worst they are reared on a specific piece of land not big enough to sustain their presence naturally, so it is overgrazed, and feed must be trucked in. This is usually manufactured pellets which rely on soya for the protein element, with often opaque supply chains for this and all other nutrients. Higher than natural levels of ticks and fleas are common problems, as is antibiotic use to prevent diseases amid the high animal densities.

In contrast parkland venison is reared in a model that mimics the wild herd behaviours. The animals roam expansive estates with mixed habitats of woodland and open areas, eat a natural diet and can play out all their natural behaviours such as fawn nesting and stag succession. The herds are closely observed and the social dynamics understood so culling is highly selective. It avoids the alpha and beta stags or other keystone individuals whose disappearance would disrupt the herd stability and instead focuses on those of a certain bodyweight and age which produces the best meat in a considered manner.

The best wild deer culling is managed in the same way, with the added benefit of producing food from unfarmable land that we need to protect for biodiversity, such as woods and valleys. The herds may be free to roam without borders of any kind, but just one or two stalkers will track, observe and understand the herd dynamics in the same way. These people are incredibly skilled and are a vital part of the farming community as they shadow the migration of herds across land ownership boundaries for the good of all. As the stalkers have to work at a distance it takes great expertise to assess the health, social status and age of each animal. They have an innate understanding of the deer and their behaviours, and it shows in the meat produced.

This is where one of the biggest arguments against venison falls down – the lack of consistency. Anonymized global food systems love consistency – it means predictable supply, fat ratios, size, weight and packaging required. Poorly culled venison may be highly variable, making it a little trickier in the kitchen, but well-managed animals produce meat that comes with no surprises, and a beautiful flavour. And so to dispel the final myth of venison, that it has a strong, unpalatable taste. By avoiding

animals in the rut, the hormones that produce this flavour are also dodged. By hanging the carcass for the right length of time for the species (shorter for red deer, longer for sika and fallow), the right balance of flavour can be landed.

Venison is also an incredibly lean meat; less than 50% the fat content of beef. Grass-fed venison has high levels of omega-6 too, known to have gold-standard health benefits for our heart and more (see Real Fat is Back, page 59 for more on this).

In short, there couldn't be a better time to start eating well-managed venison again, from herds that move through the countryside creating habitats for all of nature by trampling, pollinating, browsing and then moving on. As we better understand the impact of agriculture, choosing to eat this delicious, largely forgotten meat from an overpopulated species with a low carbon footprint is a relatively simple calculation. And you can start gently, perhaps mixing venison mince with beef in your spag bol or burgers. Try out a steak or casserole with mushrooms to see how what grows together goes together, or go all-out

for haunch (that's the equivalent of topside in beef) for a special occasion. Venison connects our kitchens to the countryside in a way that globalized, industrial, standardized farming systems never will. Let's reclaim the glory of this homespun, delicious wild meat, and all the good things it brings.

*Choosing to eat this delicious, largely forgotten meat from an overpopulated species with a low carbon footprint is a relatively simple calculation.*

This is a next-level sandwich. It could just be one of the best sandwiches you'll ever eat. The subtle iron-rich flavour of vension is a delicious partner to earthy mushrooms and tangy blue cheese. Be sure to provide a generous amount of filling in each baguette, so that your meat to bread ratio is in balance – and don't forget to add plenty of butter that will create a luscious sauce with the venison steak juices.

# Venison, Mushroom & Blue Cheese Sandwich

## — SERVES 2 —

500g (1lb 2oz) venison haunch steaks
3–4 sprigs of fresh thyme, leaves picked
1 tablespoon olive oil
2 onions, sliced
300g (10½oz) chestnut mushrooms, sliced
a few sprigs of parsley, chopped
1 large or 2 smaller fresh-baked baguettes
salted grass-fed butter, for spreading
200g (7oz) blue cheese
pure sea salt and freshly ground black pepper

Preheat the oven to 180°C/350°F/gas mark 4.

Set a large pan over a high heat. Season the venison steaks with salt and pepper and sprinkle over the thyme leaves. Set the steaks aside while you prepare the onions.

Place a large, heavy-based pan over a medium–high heat. Add the olive oil and, when it's hot, add the onions and plenty of salt and pepper. Get the onions sizzling, then reduce the heat and cook, stirring regularly, for 15–20 minutes or until they are soft and beginning to caramelize around the edges. Turn the onions out on to a plate.

Add a dash more oil to the pan, then scatter in the mushrooms. Season well and cook, tossing them round the pan, for 6–8 minutes. Return the onions to the pan and stir through the chopped parsley. Keep the mushrooms and onions warm while you cook the steak.

Pop the baguettes in the oven to warm up.

Set a griddle pan over a high heat and, when it's super hot, lay the steaks down carefully in the pan. Cook for 2–3 minutes on each side.

Remove the baguettes from the oven. Split and butter them generously. Carve the venison steaks into 2cm- (¾in)-thick slices and arrange over the buttered baguette. Spoon over the mushrooms and onions, followed by crumbly pieces of blue cheese. Serve straight away.

Deer enjoy a natural, wholesome diet and their meat is healthy, lean and full of flavour. There is often some trepidation when it comes to cooking venison, but we're here to encourage you, it really is no different to any other meat, equally as versatile and as forgiving. Here, the minced meat from the shoulder is a great alternative to a more traditional beef cottage pie.

# Forager's Pie

— SERVES 6 —

2 tablespoons olive oil
250g (9oz) wild or cultivated
    mushrooms, small ones
    left whole and larger
    ones roughly chopped
3–4 sprigs of thyme,
    leaves picked
250g (9oz) smoked
    bacon lardons
4–6 juniper berries, crushed
1 large onion, chopped
2 garlic cloves, sliced
750g (1lb 10oz) venison mince
a splash of sloe gin or brandy
1 teaspoon tomato purée
500ml (18fl oz) game,
    chicken or beef stock
    (see pages 21 and 22)
1 medium celeriac, weighing
    about 500g (1lb 2oz)
800g (1lb 12oz) white potatoes,
    such as Maris Piper or
    King Edward
4 bay leaves
100ml (3½fl oz) whole
    grass-fed milk
50g (1¾oz) grass-fed butter
2 tablespoons lightly bashed
    blanched hazelnuts
pure sea salt and freshly
    ground black pepper

Heat a large, heavy-based frying pan over a medium heat. Add the oil and, when it's hot, add the mushrooms. Sprinkle over half the thyme leaves and season them well with salt and pepper. Cook the mushrooms until they have given up their moisture and are nice and tender. Lift the mushrooms out of the pan and set to one side.

Return the pan to the heat, add the bacon lardons and crushed juniper. Sizzle them for 3–4 minutes until they start to release some of their fat. Now add the onion and garlic and continue to cook until the onion begins to soften and smells lovely and sweet. Crumble in the venison mince and season everything really well with salt and pepper. Cook the venison mince for 6–8 minutes or until it starts to brown a little. Add the sloe gin followed by the tomato purée and stock. Bring to a gentle simmer and cook, uncovered, for 45 minutes–1 hour.

Meanwhile, peel and cube the celeriac and potatoes, put them in a large saucepan, add the bay leaves and cover with plenty of salted water. Bring to the boil and simmer until the celeriac and potatoes are tender. Drain the celeriac and potatoes through a colander and leave them to steam off for a few minutes. Return the pan to a low heat and add the milk and butter. When it's hot, tumble the veg back into the pan and bash it up really well with a potato masher. Season the mash with plenty of salt and pepper and set aside.

Preheat the oven to 200°C/400°F/gas mark 6.

Stir the mushrooms through the venison, check the seasoning, then take the pan off the heat. Once the filling has cooled a little, spoon it into a large baking dish. Level it off, then carefully dot the mash all over the top until it's evenly covered. Scatter the bashed hazelnuts over the mash and sprinkle over the remaining thyme leaves. Place the dish in the middle of the oven and bake for 20–25 minutes or until the mash is crisping and golden and the filling is beginning to bubble down the sides of the dish. Serve with buttered leeks and cabbage.

With really good ingredients gathered together while they are in their seasonal prime, drenched in excellent cider – and proper cream – it's not surprising that this recipe is such a family favourite. It looks lovely all served up in one pan, ready for the serving spoon to be wrestled over and the contents merrily sloshed into bowls around the kitchen table.

# Pork, Apples, Leeks & Cider

## — SERVES 4 —

50g (1¾oz) grass-fed butter
650g (1lb 7oz) leeks, cut into 3cm (1¼in) lengths
2 apples
1 tablespoon stoneground unbleached white flour
500ml (18fl oz) cider
100ml (3½fl oz) cider brandy (we like Somerset Cider Brandy Co Kingston Black Apple Aperitif), plus extra for the apples
6 sprigs of thyme, plus leaves from 2 more sprigs to serve
4 x 125g (4½oz) native breed pork neck steaks
a drizzle of olive oil
150ml (5fl oz) double cream
pure sea salt and freshly ground black pepper

Place a heavy frying pan over a medium heat. Add the half the butter and all the leeks to the pan. Sauté them without browning for about 10 minutes; they should just soft but not sloppy.

Peel an apple, core it, halve it and cut it into wedges. Melt the remaining butter in a small frying pan and gently brown the wedges on each side until they are beautifully caramelized. Set to one side.

Add the flour to the leeks and turn them over in the juices. Take the pan off the heat and slowly add the cider and cider brandy, stirring all the time to create a lovely glossy sauce. Return the pan to the heat, bring to the boil, then add the sprigs of thyme and the sautéed apple. Immediately reduce the heat to a simmer, put the lid on and leave to cook over a low heat for about 15 minutes.

Place a frying pan over a high heat. Season the pork steaks and add to the pan with a drizzle of olive oil. Cook the pork steaks on each side for 3–4 minutes, ensuring the outside of the steaks have turned golden brown and are beautifully caramelized. Once cooked set to one side to rest.

Peel, core and cut the other apple into wedges and put in the frying pan in which you cooked the pork steaks. Saute gently, adding a further slosh of the cider brandy to help the slices caramelize nicely on the outside. Cook the apple wedges until they are just are tender.

To the leek and apple casserole, add the cream, bring to the boil and cook for a couple of minutes. Then add the pork steaks to the pan along with the just-tender caramelized apples. Sprinkle over some thyme and serve.

A true classic that makes the perfect mid-week meal. We have spruced up this family favourite by adding some beautiful squash to give you an extra portion of delicious veg, making the meat go even further. Serve with lashings of onion gravy and you have the ultimate crowd-pleasing dish.

# Toad in the Hole with Sausages, Squash, Cheddar & Onion Gravy

— SERVES 4 —

*For the batter*
140g (5oz) stoneground
    unbleached white flour
4 free-range and/or organic
    eggs, lightly beaten
200ml (7fl oz) whole
    grass-fed milk
2 tablespoons pure lard

*For the filling*
½ squash, such as butternut
    or Crown Prince, peeled
    and cut into wedges
6 pork sausages
olive oil
1 small bunch of rosemary
2 garlic cloves, finely sliced
100g (3½oz) smoked Cheddar
    cheese, crumbled
pure sea salt and freshly
    ground black pepper

*For the gravy*
olive oil
2 onions, finely sliced
2 tablespoons miso paste
    (we like Hodmedod's Fava
    Bean Umami Paste)
2 teaspoons Worcestershire
    sauce
100ml (3½fl oz) water

Preheat the oven to 200°C/400°F/gas mark 6.

To make the batter, add the flour to a mixing bowl with a good pinch of salt and pepper. Add the eggs and gently whisk in the milk to form a smooth batter. Set aside to rest for 30 minutes.

Place the squash wedges in a wide baking tray with the sausages, a drizzle of olive oil, rosemary, garlic and some salt and pepper. Bake for 25 minutes until the squash is tender and the sausages are cooked.

To the roasting tin filled with squash and sausages, add the lard and place in the oven to heat up for about 5 minutes. When the tray is very hot, add the batter and quickly return to the oven. Bake for 30 minutes. Five minutes before the toad in the hole is ready, sprinkle over the Cheddar and return to the oven to melt and bubble.

To make the gravy, add a drizzle of olive oil to a pan over a medium heat and slowly cook the onions for about 25 minutes until fully softened and lightly golden. Then add the miso paste, Worcestershire sauce and water to the onions. Bring to the boil and season with pepper.

Serve the toad in the hole with the onion gravy and some seasonal greens.

Nestled across the county on the rather beautifully named Burrow Hill you'll find the world-famous Somerset Cider Brandy Co. The farm has been pressing cider for over 200 years, and for the last 30, this family-run business has been reviving the ancient art of Somerset cider brandy production, creating some of the finest tipple in the world, including our favourite Kingston Black. In the autumn over 40 varieties of vintage and rare cider apples, such as Dabinett, Kingston Black, Stoke Red, Yarlington Mill and Harry Masters, are harvested and pressed, capturing the flavours of this traditional cider-making landscape. This recipe is really an ode to cider-making country and to the good people who for centuries have toiled on and tended to the apple orchards that make this part of the world feel like home. Here is a taste of home.

# Chicken Thighs with Kingston Black Cider Brandy & Black Pudding

— SERVES 4 —

6 properly free-range boneless chicken thighs, skin on
1 teaspoon organic rapeseed oil
1 medium onion, sliced
5 bay leaves
250ml (9fl oz) Somerset Cider Brandy Co Kingston Black Apple Aperitif
100ml (3½fl oz) chicken stock (see page 21)
150g (5½oz) black pudding
100ml (3½fl oz) double cream
a pinch of pure sea salt

Preheat the oven to 180°C/350°F/gas mark 4.

Season the chicken thighs all over with a good pinch of salt. In a cast-iron frying pan or casserole dish, heat the oil and add the chicken thighs, skin-side down. Cook for 3–4 minutes until the skin is beautifully crispy and golden brown. Flip over and cook the other side for about a minute, simply to seal the chicken and lightly brown it. Remove the chicken thighs from the pan and set to one side.

Reduce the heat under the pan and add the onions and bay leaves. Gently cook the onion in the chicken fat until translucent. Increase the heat to high and add the cider brandy. With a spatula, scrape the bottom of the pan to deglaze it and combine all the meaty scraps with the liquid. Add the chicken stock and reduce slightly for about 6 minutes.

Add the chicken thighs to the pan. Break the black pudding into chunks and fit snugly in and around the chicken thighs. Cook in the oven for about 25 minutes until the chicken thighs are beautifully tender. Check the liquid from time to time; if it looks a little dry, add a splash more cider brandy.

Remove from the oven and place over a medium heat. Add the cream and simmer for about 5 minutes until the sauce thickens.

Serve with buttery mashed potato and autumn greens.

# November

Steamy breath, frosted mornings and windows fogged up by cooking. Bonfires spark and embers glow, adding colour once again to a darkened sky. Activity on the farm slows as the land begins to enter its deep, regenerative sleep. We're thankful for a few hard tasks, like unfurling the silage to feed the cattle, as the graft generates welcome warmth on colder days.

With trees now free of their golden leaves, new hedges can be laid by twisting branches into submission. The scent of the gentle breakdown of foliage fills the air with its unmistakable earthy aroma.

This is not a quick-fix supper but rather one to sink into on a damp afternoon, as the slow process is all part of the pleasure. Braising beef is cut from the harder working parts of the cow, so it needs gently coaxing to become velvety soft. By slowing down and allowing the ingredients to relax and get to know one another, you'll be rewarded with rich umami flavour from the combination of beef and oyster mushrooms.

# Beef, Lovage & Oyster Mushroom Pie
## — SERVES 6 —

500g (1lb 2oz) rough puff
    pastry (see page 270)
1 free-range and/or
    organic egg, beaten
pure sea salt and freshly
    ground black pepper

*For the filling*
olive oil
500g (1lb 2oz) grass-fed
    braising beef, diced
1 onion, sliced
2 carrots, peeled and
    cut into large chunks
4 garlic cloves, crushed
500ml (18fl oz) beef stock
    (see page 22)
250ml (9fl oz) red wine
1 small bunch of rosemary,
    roughly chopped
1 tablespoon cornflour
100g (3½oz) oyster
    mushrooms
50g (1¾oz) unsalted
    grass-fed butter
1 sprig of lovage,
    leaves picked

Prehat the oven to 150°C/300°F/gas mark 2.

To make the filling, set a wide, heavy-based frying pan over a high heat, add some oil and fry the diced beef in batches until it takes on a good amount of colour. Transfer the beef to a bowl and set to one side.

Add a little more oil to the pan and fry the onion, carrots and garlic for 8 minutes until they are caramelized and just starting to soften.

Add the vegetables and beef to a large, ovenproof dish or pan along with the beef stock, red wine and rosemary. Cook in the oven for 2–3 hours until the beef is tender.

Remove the pie filling from the oven and place over a medium heat. Take a little of the beefy sauce and mix with the cornflour. Return this mixture to the pan of filling and bring to a simmer until the mixture thickens. Remove from the heat and leave to cool.

Fry the oyster mushrooms in the butter, season with salt and pepper and stir through the pie filling along with the lovage. Set aside to cool.

Transfer the cooled pie mix to a large pie dish and increase the oven temperature to 180°C/350°F/gas mark 4.

Roll out the pastry until just wider than the dish you're making the pie in. Brush the underside of the pastry sheet with beaten egg to ensure the pastry sticks to the dish. Gently place the pastry on top of the pie dish and press the pastry into the sides of the dish. Brush the top of the pastry with beaten egg and poke a steam hole in the centre of the pie to allow the steam to escape.

Bake the pie for 30–40 minutes until the pastry is golden brown and the filling is bubbling. Leave to rest for 10 minutes before digging in.

It may seem a slightly strange option, a salad in November, however this warm version is filled with deep, earthy, umami flavours. The mushrooms and the celeriac pair wonderfully together and bring flavours of the forest floor, while the bitter radicchio cuts through with sharp abandon. We have served this version with some beautifully crisp chicken breasts, sliced and strewn amongst the veg, but it works equally well with ribbons of beef steak – a bavette steak would be our preference.

# Warm Winter Chicken Salad with Celeriac, Mushrooms & Radicchio

## — SERVES 2 —

½ bulb of celeriac, peeled and
    diced into 2.cm (1in) pieces
250g (9oz) chestnut
    mushrooms, quartered
2 tablespoons pumpkin seeds
extra virgin olive oil
2 free-range chicken breasts,
    skin on
50g (1¾oz) grass-fed butter
2 sprigs of thyme
1 small head of radicchio,
    picked down to individual
    leaves and washed
a pinch of pure sea salt
pure sea salt and freshly
    ground black pepper

*For the dressing*
1 tablespoon Dijon mustard
1 tablespoon red wine vinegar
1 teaspoon sugar
2 tablespoons extra virgin olive
    oil or organic rapeseed oil

Preheat the oven to 190°C/375°F/gas mark 5.

Place the diced celeriac, mushrooms and pumpkin seeds in a baking tray and dress with a generous drizzle of olive oil, season well with salt and pepper, then roast in the oven for 20–25 minutes until the celeriac is tender. Stir the contents of the tray every 10 minutes or so to ensure they cook evenly.

While the veg is cooking, prepare the chicken. Place a medium heavy-based frying pan over a medium heat. Add a drizzle of olive oil and add the chicken breasts, skin-side down. Season the other side of the breasts with plenty of salt and pepper. Place another smaller pan on top of the chicken as it cooks, to act as a weight. This ensures the chicken skin doesn't contract and helps it become crispy.

After 5 minutes of cooking in the pan the chicken should look roughly half-cooked, at this stage add the butter and thyme and transfer to the oven, still skin-side down, for a further 5 minutes. Remove from the oven, turn skin-side up and leave to rest for 5 minutes.

Once the veg has cooked, remove from the oven and tip into a large bowl in which you can dress the salad. Add the radicchio to the celeriac and mushrooms.

In a smaller bowl, whisk together the mustard, vinegar, sugar and oil, alongside any buttery resting juices from the chicken, to form a dressing. Pour this over the radicchio and vegetables, ensuring it coats everything evenly.

Arrange the warm salad on a large platter and carve the chicken into thick slices, placing it on top of the salad. Finish with a final drizzle of olive oil and a twist of black pepper.

Sweet, sticky balsamic-laden onions relent as a fork is pressed to their soft shell, ready to be scooped up and applied to mineral-rich, herb-infused, proper ox liver... There is no doubt why this dish is a perennial favourite. A few really good ingredients, cooked simply, yielding magnificent results.

# Ox Liver with Vinegar Glazed Onions & Crispy Sage

## — SERVES 2 —

olive oil
6 small onions or shallots
3 tablespoons balsamic vinegar
250ml (9fl oz) beef stock
    (see page 22)
6 slices of ox liver, no
    thinner than 2cm (¾in)
50g (1¾oz) grass-fed butter
a small handful of sage leaves
pure sea salt and freshly
    ground black pepper

Place a frying pan over a medium heat and add a good drizzle of oil followed by the onions. Move the onions around in the pan until they have taken on lots of colour, carefully caramelizing them to bring out their sweet flavour.

Add the balsamic vinegar to the pan and reduce it until its starts to form a sticky syrup. Follow this with the beef stock and reduce by a third. Cover the pan with a lid or a layer of foil and cook over a low heat for 15–20 minutes until the onions are beautifully tender.

When the onions are nearly ready, heat a second frying pan.

Season the slices of liver with plenty of salt and pepper. When the pan is smoking hot, add the liver and cook for 1 minute on each side. Use a spatula to keep the liver flat in the pan. Add the butter and sage leaves to the pan and allow the sage to crisp. Once the sage has stopped crackling, remove the pan from the heat.

Add the liver and sage to the pan with the onions and pour the contents on to 2 plates.

Serve with buttered sourdough bread and a well-dressed green salad.

As we move into the depths of winter, the days are short and the air outside has a sharp, cold bite to it. It's during these darker months that food with depth and character is filling our hearts and minds. Slow-cooked for many hours, basically until the meat falls apart when you touch it, this stew is just the thing we need. The addition of pearled barley provides a gelatinous, starchy quality, not to mention a gorgeous nutty texture.

# Beef, Onion, Barley & Stout Stew

## — SERVES 3–4 —

1.5kg (3lb 5oz) beef shin
  on the bone
25g (1oz) grass-fed
  beef dripping
1 large or 2 smaller
  onions, sliced
4 large carrots, peeled
  and cut into chunks
4 garlic cloves, thinly sliced
2 sprigs of rosemary
350ml (12fl oz) bottle of stout
500ml (18fl oz) beef stock
  (see page 22)
100g (3½oz) pearled
  barley, rinsed
pure sea salt and freshly
  ground black pepper

Preheat the oven to 160°C/325°F/gas mark 3.

Season the beef shin with salt and pepper. Place a large, heavy-based, lidded casserole dish over a high heat. Add the beef dripping and, when it's hot, add the beef shin and fry it on all sides until it's taken on a lovely dark colour. (You might need to do this in batches.) Remove the beef from the pan.

Add the onions, carrots, garlic and the rosemary to the pan and cook, stirring constantly, for 8–10 minutes. Return the beef to the pan, pour over the stout and the stock and a splash more water to make sure you cover the meat, if necessary. Bring everything to a simmer, place a lid on the pan and set it in the middle of the oven. Cook the beef for about 3 hours or until the meat is almost tender. We like to turn the meat once or twice during this time so it all cooks evenly.

Now add the rinsed barley, give the pan a good shake so it settles below the cooking liquor, and continue to cook, with the lid on, for a further 45 minutes. If the stew looks a little dry at any point, then add a dash of water. When the meat is lovely and tender and the barley is cooked through, remove the pan from the oven. Season everything well with salt and pepper.

To serve, spoon the stew into bowls. Alternatively, let it cool for a while, then pull the meat off the bone and return it in nice generous chunks to the sauce. Reheat and serve.

Be brave with the horseradish, you want enough so that the peppery heat climbs the sinuses and brings a tear to the eye.

# Steak Sandwiches with Beetroot, Horseradish & Dill

— SERVES 2 —

½ small red onion, very finely sliced
2–3 beetroots, cooked and cut into fine matchsticks
2 tablespoons crème fraîche
1 small bunch of dill, chopped
a pinch of ground allspice
a dash of balsamic vinegar
a knob of fresh horseradish root, or 2 tablespoons creamed horseradish
olive oil
4 grass-fed beef sandwich steaks
grass-fed butter, for spreading
4 thick slices of sourdough bread
a handful of salad leaves or the beetroot tops
pure sea salt and freshly ground black pepper

In a small mixing bowl, add the onion, beetroot, crème fraîche, dill and allspice and combine. Pour in the balsamic vinegar and generously season everything with salt and pepper.

Peel the end of the horseradish root and then grate some into the bowl, about 1 tablespoon. Mix well, taste and add more horseradish to your liking; be bold.

Get a frying pan or griddle pan as searingly hot as you can. Lightly oil the steaks and season with salt and pepper. Fry them for just shy of a minute on each side until nicely coloured. Remove from the pan and leave them to rest for a few minutes.

Butter the bread and divide the salad leaves and beetroot mix between 2 slices. Top each with 2 steaks and then pop the remaining slices on top and tuck in.

As crackles and pops fill the air, warming bowls of hearty food are required to keep fingers away from Jack Frost's touch. Instead of rather more traditional bonfire fayre, we love serving up this cauldron of bubbling chilli. Once the chilli has been cooked, the embers can be used for toasting marshmallows or lighting sparklers, making your outdoor party all the more memorable.

# Spiced Pork & Carlin Pea Campfire Chilli

— SERVES 4 —

250g (9oz) bacon lardons

500g (1lb 2oz) native breed diced pork

2 red onions, diced

2 garlic cloves, crushed

2 tablespoons shawarma paste (see below)

400g (14oz) can chopped tomatoes

1 litre (1¾ pints) chicken stock (see page 21)

2 bay leaves

1 small bunch of marjoram (or any aromatic garden herb)

400g (14oz) can carlin peas, drained

pure sea salt and freshly ground black pepper

*For the shawarma paste*

1½ tablespoons dark brown sugar

1 tablespoon ground coriander

2 teaspoons ground cumin

1 teaspoon pure sea salt

1 teaspoon smoked paprika

1 teaspoon ground turmeric

½ teaspoon freshly ground black pepper

¼ teaspoon cinnamon

¼ teaspoon dried ginger

½ teaspoon chilli powder

5 medium garlic cloves, grated

3 tablespoons extra virgin olive oil

Spread a good amount of sustainable lumpwood charcoal in the base of your barbecue. Using one or two sustainable firelighters, light the coals and leave them to turn grey with flecks of red embers.

To make the shawarma paste, add all the ingredients to a bowl and mix to a paste. You can store the shawarma paste in a sterilized jam jar in the fridge for 2 weeks.

Take a sturdy casserole dish and place it directly into the coals. Once the dish is smoking hot, add the bacon lardons and fry until a good amount of bacon fat has been released and the lardons have become crisp and golden. Then add the diced pork and fry for 5–10 minutes until the pork has browned.

Add the onions, garlic and shawarma paste and gently fry for a further few minutes until the onions have started to soften. The spice mix will generously coat the meat and give off a wonderfully nutty scent. Next, into the dish go the tomatoes and half the stock, along with the bay leaves and marjoram.

Remove the casserole dish from the direct heat by hanging it over your barbecue using a chain. Gently simmer the pot over the heat for 1–2 hours, adding more stock when necessary. You will need to top up the charcoal to ensure you have a fairly consistent cooking heat.

Finally, add the carlin peas and simmer for a further 10 minutes.

Season to taste and serve in deep bowls either by itself or with tangy soured cream or why not roast some baking potatoes in the embers of the fire and load them with chilli and cheese?

This is a properly rustic and hearty bowl of soup. It's very easy to put together, with most of the component parts able to be interchanged for similar counterparts. For instance, the bacon could be replaced by homemade chorizo, or the kale could be swapped for spring greens. The beans aren't demanding either, they could be replaced with butter, borlotti or even chickpeas. The principle works no matter what you have foraged from your larder.

# Bacon, Kale & Bean Soup

## — SERVES 2 —

300g (10½ oz) bacon lardons
2 onions, finely chopped
3 garlic cloves, chopped
1 litre (1¾ pints) chicken
    stock (see page 21)
1 teaspoon smoked paprika
100g (3½oz) passata
2 bay leaves
400g (14oz) can cannellini
    beans, drained
100g (3½oz) cavolo nero
    or kale, stalks removed
    and chopped
extra virgin olive oil
pure sea salt and freshly
    ground black pepper

Heat a large casserole dish on the hob. Fry the lardons until they take on a lovely golden colour and have crisped up. Add the chopped onions and garlic to the pan and gently cook until the onions are soft and sweet.

Add the chicken stock, smoked paprika and passata. Bring to a gentle simmer and then add the bay leaves. Gently simmer it all together for about 20 minutes.

Add the cannellini beans and cavolo nero and simmer for a further 5 minutes. Taste the soup and add salt and pepper as required.

Drizzle with your best olive oil and serve with toasted sourdough.

# December

Outside on the hills it is so quiet, the wing of a buzzard can be heard as it glides up above in search of a juicy earthworm, or perhaps, if it's lucky, an unfortunate mouse. The silence is broken only by the clatter of unearthed wild deer as they take off from the thicket into open pasture.

The farmhouse comes into its own in preparation for winter and Christmas. The fireplace draws all near, thawing fingers after chilly work. The kitchen table sees us share wreath and pudding-making tasks over warm conversation in good company. We look ahead to gatherings where we will share the good food and simple, natural things we have lovingly crafted over the year.

# How to Have a Pipers Farm Christmas

Christmas is such a wonderful time of year. It's a comforting, reflective time, a time to slow down, to be at home and cook delicious things to eat.

For over 30 years we have been helping families around the country create magical Christmas memories by carefully rearing magnificent food fit for the finest celebration. Of all the meals we cook throughout the year, there is no question that the festive feast is the most important one.

Every family has their own way of celebrating the day. They'll have their own little traditions that make it feel unique to them. In many homes, roast turkey takes centre stage. For some families, Christmas just isn't Christmas without a glazed ham or a handsome rib of beef. No matter what the centrepiece of choice may be, one thing is for certain, it must be reared properly, trussed beautifully and delivered to the door ready to be lovingly adorned for the Christmas table – and that's a job we take very seriously.

We start our planning for the festivities, would you believe it, in February. We need to decide how many chicks we plan to hatch that will spend the next 7–8 months maturing into plump turkeys and geese for the table. Legs of pork that are destined to become luscious gammons start to be laid down ready for brining in the early summer. Ribs of beef start to be squirrelled away from July, to build a store that can fulfil our wonderful customers' requirements. In September our dedicated army of sausage makers begin the arduous task of hand-making tens of thousands of the

nation's favourite 'pigs in blankets', the adorable bacon-wrapped chipolatas that so admirably accompany a roast bird, by hand-rolling each sausage into its cuddly blanket and tucking it up in the freezer until the big day. You see, in order to provide those special ingredients that make majestic meals, precision and planning are paramount.

When it comes to preparing Christmas meals to remember at home, the same rules apply, as planning and preparation really do take the angst away and help make this a season filled with magical moments and memories.

Get your centrepiece order – whether bird, beef or something else – placed with your butcher or farmer nice and early and mark the collection or delivery date in your calendar.

Plan your festive menu as best you can, around who's coming and when – making sure you have a few treats tucked away in case unexpected guests show up (our recipe for Boozy Sausage Rolls on page 273 is perfect for this). This will also help you to avoid aimlessly buying food from the supermarket for the sake of it and ending up with mountains of waste. Plan meals that can be made ahead and frozen (our Beef & Barley Stew on page 235 is a godsend, hidden away in the freezer, to be thawed and served in a flash). This allows you more time to wrap presents and challenge loved ones to a game of Monopoly. After all, Christmas shouldn't be about being chained to the stove, it's about being together and creating memories that last a lifetime.

# How to Roast a Turkey

Every family has their own way of celebrating Christmas Day. They'll have their rituals and idiosyncrasies that make Christmas feel truly personal, but one thing that is shared is that Christmas dinner must be delicious! Thankfully, we are on hand to share our tried and tested recipe to make sure your lovingly reared Christmas turkey is cooked to perfection.

1 free-range bronze turkey
a selection of fresh herbs
    (we like thyme, rosemary
    and bay leaves)
2 bulbs of garlic, halved
4 onions, halved
pure sea salt

Preheat the oven to 180°C/350°F/gas mark 4.

It is really important to take your turkey out of the fridge nice and early on the day you plan to cook it. You want to allow it to come up to room temperature so the meat isn't shocked when you place it in the oven.

Pat the turkey dry with kitchen paper and place it into a suitably sized roasting dish. If the legs overhang, simply wrap a bit of foil around them and build a trench channelling any liquid back into the dish.

Generously season the turkey all over, making sure you have rubbed a good amount of salt into all the areas of the bird, including inside the cavity.

Inside the tray, surround the turkey with fresh herbs, garlic and the halved onions. (These additions will provide a bouquet of aromatics that will infuse your bird as it cooks, and also help make the most incredible gravy when combined with the turkey dish juices.)

Cook the turkey for 20–25 minutes per 1kg (2lb 4oz). If you are stuffing your bird, simply add the weight of the stuffing to the weight of your bird and calculate the total weight and cooking time.

The best indication that your bird is cooked is when it's easy to shake hands with it. Grab a tea towel or an oven glove and gently twist the drumstick to the side. As soon as it 'gives' this is the best indication the bird is cooked. You can also put a skewer into the thickest part of the thigh – the juices should run slightly pink.

Remove the turkey from the oven and leave to rest somewhere warm for about 30 minutes to allow all of the juices to settle and stay in the bird.

Serve with roast potatoes, homemade gravy and seasonal vegetables (see page 267).

We are entrusting you with our handed-down family recipe for roast goose.
Use it and enjoy many happy memories with your loved ones at Christmas time.

# Roast Goose with Prune, Bacon & Chestnut Stuffing

— SERVES 6 —

4–5kg (9–11lb) free-range goose
Prune, Bacon & Chestnut
   Stuffing (see page 268)
25g (1oz) grass-fed butter,
   softened
1 tablespoon pure sea salt
1 tablespoon freshly ground
   black pepper
a small bouquet of garden herbs
   (we like thyme, rosemary,
   sage and bay leaves)

*To serve*
Proper Gravy (see page 267)
The Best Roast Potatoes
   (see page 267)

It is really important to take your goose out of the fridge early on the day you plan to cook it. You want to allow it to come up to room temperature so the meat isn't shocked when you place it in the oven.

Using some kitchen paper, pat the goose dry and ensure there isn't any liquid lingering in the cavity. Pull the wings and legs away from the goose – this allows the heat to circulate around the bird. With a skewer or the tip of a sharp knife, pierce the fattiest parts of the goose, being careful only to puncture the fat and not the flesh.

To stuff the goose, spoon the stuffing into the neck cavity end, pressing it in as far as you can and then tucking the neck skin all around it and shaping it nicely with your hands. Secure the skin underneath with a skewer or a couple of cocktail sticks. Rub the goose all over with the butter and season all over with the salt and pepper. Place the bouquet of herbs in the cavity. Transfer the goose to a wire rack and then place the wire rack into a large roasting dish. It is important to do this due to the copious amounts of fat in a properly free-range goose, otherwise the heat cannot penetrate the entire bird and it will stew in its fat.

Roast the goose in the middle of the hot oven for 40 minutes. Reduce the temperature to 180°C/350°F/gas mark 4 and cook for a further 1½ hours, basting occasionally. At this point check the internal temperature of the goose. The breast should be about 60°C (140°F) but if you like your bird well done, cook it until it reaches 72°C (162°F).

Now carefully remove the goose to a large plate, cover and keep warm. Spoon out the hot fat (keep this in a jar in the fridge for next time or use to make The Best Roast Potatoes on page 267), then set about making the Proper Gravy (see page 267).

To carve the goose, remove the whole breast first, carefully slicing down each side of the breastbone with a sharp knife and gently easing the breasts away from the goose. Slice the breast across the grain into thick pieces. Then take the legs off at the base of the thighs and carve these in a more traditional way. Serve the goose with the stuffing, gravy, roast potatoes and some buttered greens.

A good roast duck at Christmas time has become increasingly popular among our customers with many smaller families opting not to take on the vastness of a whole goose, but still wanting some of that delightfully sweet, rich meat that we all crave so much during the festivities. Enter a plump, properly reared duck that has been hung and trussed ready for the table. The juices from the fat of the bird are a delight, they can be soaked up by a stuffing, or tipped out to make the most delicious gravy.

# Roast Duck with
# Quince & Brussels Sprouts

— SERVES 5 —

2 teaspoons juniper berries
2 teaspoons coriander seeds
1 sprig of rosemary,
    leaves picked
2.5kg (5lb 8oz)
    free-range duck
1 teaspoon olive oil
4 quince, quartered
400g (14oz) Brussels
    sprouts, halved
pure sea salt and freshly
    ground black pepper

Preheat the oven to 180°C/350°F/gas mark 4.

In a pestle and mortar, grind the juniper berries, coriander seeds, rosemary, some black pepper and a good pinch of salt.

Place the duck in a roasting dish, drizzle with the olive oil and rub it into the skin. Sprinkle the spice mix over the duck and massage this into the skin of the duck too.

Roast the duck for 55 minutes, then add the quince and sprouts, generously coating the fruit and vegetables in the luscious duck fat. Return to the oven and roast for a further 25 minutes.

Remove the dish from the oven and leave the duck to rest for about 15 minutes to allow the juices to set.

Carve and serve the duck with a generous helping of the roast quince and sprouts.

Good beef speaks for itself. It doesn't need much, a pinch of salt, a crack of black pepper and a hot oven are all it really takes. Be sure not to overcook it – please eat it rare, or at least medium-rare, that is what this beast deserves.

# Rib of Beef with Braised Red Cabbage

## — SERVES 8–9 —

1 large rib of beef, weighing
    4.5kg (9lb 13oz)
2 onions, quartered
4 sprigs of rosemary
4 sprigs of thyme
6 bay leaves
pure sea salt and freshly
    ground black pepper

*For the braised red cabbage*
olive oil
1 red cabbage, sliced
50g (1¾oz) redcurrant jelly
50ml (2fl oz) cider vinegar
50ml (2fl oz) dark soy sauce

Remove the rib of beef from the fridge well before you plan on cooking it, ideally a minimum of 4 hours beforehand.

To make the braised red cabbage, set a large casserole dish over a medium heat and add a good drizzle of oil, then the red cabbage. Add the redcurrant jelly, cider vinegar and soy sauce. Gently cook with a lid on for 45 minutes–1 hour or until the cabbage is softened and has absorbed all the flavours from the seasonings.

Preheat the oven to 220°C/425°F/gas mark 7.

Take the widest pan you have and set over a high heat. Season the rib with lots of salt and pepper. Place the rib, fat-side down, in the pan and begin to render the fat. With a large piece of meat like a rib this process will take time, so prepare to be patient. Regularly move the rib around the pan and drain the beef fat away at regular intervals. The end result you are aiming for is a beautiful golden brown layer of fat around the rib – this may take 20–30 minutes.

Transfer the rib to a baking dish that will snugly hold it. Add the onions and herbs and place in the oven for 20 minutes.

Reduce the oven temperature to 160°C/325°F/gas mark 3.

Calculating cooking times for a large piece of meat can be a challenge and one we often resolve by using a digital temperature probe to keep track of how the meat is cooking. For rare aim for an internal temperature of 48–50°C (118–122°F) and for medium 55–60°C (131–140°F). If you don't have a temperature probe, calculate the cooking time based on the weight of your rib of beef. For every 500g (1lb 2oz) of meat it will need roughly 10 minutes for rare, 20 minutes for medium and 30 minutes for well done.

Once you are happy that your rib of beef is cooked to your liking, leave to rest at room temperature for a minimum of 30 minutes before carving with a sharp knife and serving with the cabbage.

Rich, creamy, crunchy-topped leeks work so wonderfully with roast beef. Leeks and beef are just so good together. In this particular recipe, we've added a handful of dried cep mushrooms. They give the gratin an extra dimension that is needed for a celebratory meal; their uniquely wonderful earthy flavour is no stranger to beef.

# Roast Boneless Rib of Beef with Leek, Cep & Parsley Gratin

## — SERVES 6 —

*For the gratin*
4–5 medium leeks, trimmed and roughly chopped
850ml (1½ pints) whole grass-fed milk
a handful of flat-leaf parsley, leaves picked and chopped, stalks retained
2 bay leaves
100g (3½oz) unsalted grass-fed butter
25g (1oz) dried cep mushrooms
2 garlic cloves, thinly sliced
50g (1¾oz) stoneground unbleached white flour
75g (2¾oz) mature Cheddar cheese
1 heaped teaspoon Dijon mustard
½ small bunch of thyme, leaves picked
a handful of coarse, stale white breadcrumbs
pure sea salt and freshly ground black pepper

*For the beef*
olive oil or grass-fed beef dripping
1.5kg (3lb 5oz) boneless rib of grass-fed beef
100g (3½oz) grass-fed butter
1 medium bunch of thyme
3–4 garlic cloves

Preheat the oven to 200°C/400°F/gas mark 6.

Place the leeks in a pan and pour over the milk. Add the parsley stalks and bay leaves. Place the pan over a medium heat, bring to a simmer and immediately turn off the heat. Leave the milk to infuse.

Place another large pan over a medium heat. Melt 25g (1oz) of the butter and, then add the leeks, cep mushrooms and garlic and season lightly with salt and pepper. Add 3–4 tablespoons of water and place a lid on the pan. Let the leeks steam gently for 10–12 minutes or until tender.

Melt the remaining butter in another large pan over a medium heat, then stir in the flour. Reduce the heat to medium–low and cook gently for a minute or so, then pour half the infused milk through a sieve into the pan. Whisk the sauce vigorously, then strain in the remaining milk and whisk again. Add all but a handful of the cheese along with the mustard, thyme leaves and chopped parsley and stir well. Taste and season with salt and plenty of black pepper. Finally, fold in the steamed leeks and mushrooms. Set to one side.

Heat a large, heavy-based frying pan over a medium–high heat. Add some oil or beef dripping and, when it's nice and hot, season the beef well and carefully lay it in the pan. Fry the beef on all sides until golden.

Add the butter to the pan, then the thyme sprigs and garlic. Use a spoon to baste the beef with the butter. Spend a few minutes doing this, it'll really carry the flavour of the thyme and garlic on to the beef. Transfer the beef, garlic and thyme to a roasting tray and cook for 45 minutes–1 hour or until the beef has an internal temperature of 50–55°C (122–131°F) for medium-rare or 60°C (140°F) if you like it cooked for a little longer. Loosely cover the beef and rest somewhere warm for 15–20 minutes.

While the beef rests, spoon the leek and cep mixture into a large ovenproof dish. Scatter over the breadcrumbs and remaining cheese and bake for 12–15 minutes, or until bubbling and golden.

There are many moments of celebration dotted throughout the winter calendar and last-minute guests doing the rounds weeks before the big day. You'll need to be armed with a few celebratory recipes that will welcome and spoil – and feel right for the time of year. This is one of those recipes, impressive, but most of all delicious. For those wanting to shake up tradition, venison makes a wonderful alternative to turkey.

# Roast Saddle of Venison with Prune, Bacon & Chestnut Stuffing

— SERVES 6–8 —

4–6 sheets of caul fat,
   soaked in water for
   5 minutes
12–16 sage leaves
2.5–3kg (5lb 8oz–6lb 8oz)
   saddle of venison
Prune Bacon & Chestnut
   Stuffing (see page 268)

Preheat the oven to 200°C fan/400°F/gas mark 6.

Remove the caul fat from the water and lay it out over a large chopping board or clean work surface, overlapping the sheets so that they form a surface area large enough to envelop the entire saddle once stuffed.

Scatter over the sage leaves randomly, then place 4–5 lengths of butcher's string, each around 50cm (20in) long, over the caul at an even distance apart.

Lay the venison on top of the fat and string, skin-side down, then spoon the stuffing down the centre between the two loins, shaping it with your hands into an even sausage.

Arrange the fillets, if they are loose, alongside too. Fold in the sides of the venison to encase the stuffing as neatly and evenly as you can. Now bring up the pieces of string and tie them off to secure the rolled meat. Lift the fat over the venison in neatly ordered folds. Carefully lift the saddle and turn it over and place into a large roasting tray.

Place the venison in the oven and roast for 15–20 minutes, then reduce the temperature to 180°C/350°F/gas mark 4 and continue to cook for a further 40 minutes, or until a digital temperature probe pushed into the joint reaches 60°C (140°F), for medium-rare meat. Remove the venison, cover and leave it to rest for 15 minutes.

Serve with roast potatoes and gravy (see page 267).

Roasting a larger piece of meat than one needs may seem wasteful but, in fact, it's the opposite. Cold pork makes marvellous meat to be sliced and served cold the next day. It's good-sense cooking, using the oven once while providing multiple meals. This may help you during the festive season when you can feel like all you have seen are the kitchen walls.

# Roast Pork Loin with Root Vegetables

— SERVES 7 —

600g (1lb 5oz) carrots, peeled and sliced into long pieces
600g (1lb 5oz) parsnips, peeled
olive oil
1 teaspoon smoked paprika
1 tablespoon coriander seeds, bashed
1 teaspoon cumin seeds
1 tablespoon honey
1kg (2lb 4oz) pork loin, rind scored
pure sea salt and freshly ground black pepper

Preheat the oven to 200°C/400°F/gas mark 6.

Add the carrots and parsnips to a large baking tray and season with plenty of olive oil, salt and pepper along with the smoked paprika and coriander and cumin seeds. Mix well by hand, cover the tray tightly with a layer of foil and bake for 25 minutes.

Remove the foil, add the honey and return to the oven for a further 15 minutes.

Increase the oven temperature to 220°C/425°F/gas mark 7.

Season the pork with salt. Place on a baking tray and roast for 15 minutes to give the crackling a head start.

Reduce the oven temperature to 180°C/350°F/gas mark 4 and roast the pork for 30 minutes, or until the pork reaches an internal temperature of 60–65°C (140–149°F), if using a digital temperature probe.

Leave to rest uncovered for 20 minutes at room temperature.

Serve the pork with the carrots and parsnips and any other roast trimmings you may want, such as roast potatoes, Yorkshire puddings and gravy (see pages 267–8).

Other than a plump bird, there is no greater centrepiece at Christmas time than a lovingly glazed gammon. It is a thing of beauty. The shining star of the Christmas banquet. Glazing the gammon with something sticky and sweet is a vital part of the ritual. The balance of sweet and mustard heat can be tweaked exactly as you wish.

# Glazed Ham

## — SERVES 20 —

8kg (17lb 8oz) rare breed
  unsmoked gammon
150ml (5fl oz) dark soy sauce
150g (5½oz) Dijon mustard
150g (5½oz) honey
150ml (5fl oz) cider vinegar
1 tablespoon of cloves

It takes about 2 days to prepare this handsome joint, so do plan plenty of time. Before you intend to cook the gammon, place the joint in the sink, cover it with water and leave to soak overnight.

Place gammon in an ovenproof casserole dish that is big enough to completely submerge it and fill the dish with fresh water. Place over a medium heat and gently bring to the boil, then reduce the heat to a very gentle simmer – the pan should be just 'blipping' away. Leave the gammon to gently simmer for 5–6 hours, however, this could take longer depending on the exact shape of the gammon and the volume of water you are cooking it in. The best way to check whether your gammon is cooked to perfection is by using a digital temperature probe. Place the probe into the thickest part of the joint, avoiding any bones. You are looking to achieve a temperature of 65–70°C (149–158°F).

Remove from the heat and leave the gammon, which we can refer to as 'ham' now it is cooked, to cool in the cooking liquid, ideally overnight.

To prepare the glaze, simmer the soy sauce, Dijon mustard, honey and cider vinegar together in a saucepan over a low heat.

Preheat the oven to 160°C/325°F/gas mark 3.

When the ham has completely cooled, remove it from the pan and carefully remove the skin. To do this, take a sharp knife and place the blade above the fat and directly under the skin and, using smooth movements and keeping the blade pointed towards the skin, cut the skin away without taking the fat along with it. The fat should be set hard, so you can 'criss-cross' the fat with 2.5cm (1in) deep cuts. Pierce each square of fat with a clove. Place the ham in a roasting tray and cover the fat with the glaze. Cook in the oven for 4 hours, removing every 30 minutes or so to baste the ham with the juices from the pan.

Remove the ham from the oven and leave to rest for about 20 minutes. Slice and serve with crusty sourdough, seasonal pickles and an array of farmhouse cheeses.

Some might argue, the best part of a roast dinner...

# Trimmings

## Proper Gravy

**SERVES 4–6**

---

2 tablespoons stoneground unbleached white flour
180ml (6fl oz) white wine
500ml (18fl oz) beef or chicken stock
  (see pages 21 and 22)
2 teaspoons red wine vinegar
1 tablespoon redcurrant jelly
pure sea salt and freshly ground black pepper

*The veg from your roasting tray*
1 onion, quartered
2 carrots, peeled and roughly chopped
2 celery sticks, roughly chopped
4 garlic cloves, bashed
2 bay leaves
3–4 sprigs of thyme

---

Remove the roast meat from the roasting tray and set it aside.

Place the roasting tray, full of all the delicious fat, juices and vegetables, over a medium heat. Sprinkle in the flour and work this into the contents. Cook gently for 1–2 minutes.

Crush the veg with the back of a spoon and scrape at any dark sticky patches on the bottom of the tray.

Add the wine along with the stock. Bring the gravy to a simmer and cook gently for 15–20 minutes, stirring regularly.

Pass the gravy through a fine sieve into a clean saucepan, pressing all the flavour out of the meat and vegetables with the back of the spoon or ladle as you go. Set the pan over a low heat and add the red wine vinegar and redcurrant jelly, stir well and season.

## The Best Roast Potatoes

**SERVES 6**

---

1.5kg (3lb 5oz) large-ish Maris Piper (or other white floury)
  potatoes, peeled and cut into large-ish pieces
150g (5½oz) grass-fed beef dripping, free-range goose
  fat or native breed pork lard
1 small bulb of garlic, separated and lightly bashed
3–4 sprigs of rosemary, torn
4–5 sprigs of fresh thyme, leaves picked
pure sea salt and freshly ground black pepper

---

Preheat the oven to 200°C/400°F/gas mark 6.

Rinse the potatoes in several changes of cold water to help remove excess starch. Place in a large saucepan, cover with plenty of salted water and bring to the boil. Reduce the heat and simmer for 8–10 minutes or until they are just tender. Drain in a colander, then allow them to steam off for at least 5–10 minutes. Tumble the potatoes around in the colander to rough up their edges and make them even crispier.

Meanwhile, spoon the fat into a large, heavy-based baking tray and place it in the oven to heat up. When it's hot, carefully turn the potatoes out into the tray. Use a spatula to turn them through the fat, then make sure they've all got a little space. Sprinkle them all over with salt and pepper. Roast in the middle of the oven for 25–30 minutes, turning once. Lift the tray out of the oven and carefully squish the potatoes lightly. Add the garlic, rosemary and thyme and turn together. Cook for a further 25–30 minutes or until the potatoes are lovely and crisp and golden. Use a slotted spatula to lift the potatoes on to a large plate, sprinkle with some extra salt and serve.

# Yorkshire Puddings

**MAKES 12**

---

140g (5oz) stoneground unbleached white flour
4 free-range and/or organic eggs
200ml (7fl oz) grass-fed milk
3 tablespoons grass-fed beef dripping
pure sea salt and freshly ground black pepper

---

Preheat the oven to 230°C/450°F/gas mark 8.

To make the batter, add the flour to a mixing bowl, make a well in the centre, add the eggs and beat together until smooth. Gradually add the milk and carry on beating until the mixture is completely lump-free. Season with salt and pepper. We like to rest the batter for about an hour before using, but you don't have to do this.

Take a 12-hole cupcake tray and divide the beef dripping equally between the holes and place in the oven to heat the fat.

Carefully remove the tray of hot fat from the oven. Quickly and evenly pour the batter into the holes. Place the tray back in the oven and leave undisturbed for 25–30 minutes until the puddings have puffed up and browned.

# Prune, Bacon & Chestnut Stuffing

**SERVES 6**

---

25g (1oz) grass-fed butter, softened
150g (5½oz) streaky bacon, finely diced
2 shallots, finely diced
150g (5½oz) prunes, pitted and roughly chopped
200g (7oz) cooked chestnuts, peeled and roughly chopped
zest of 1 lemon
1 small bunch of sage
300g (10½oz) sausage meat
pure sea salt and freshly ground black pepper

---

Place a medium frying pan over a medium heat. Add the butter and, when it's bubbling away, add the bacon. Sizzle the bacon for about 6 minutes until it starts to crisp up a little. Then scatter in the diced shallots and fry gently, stirring regularly, for 6–8 minutes until they are translucent. Pour the bacon and shallots into a mixing bowl.

Add the prunes, chestnuts, lemon zest and sage and stir well. Season everything generously with salt and pepper and set aside to cool before mixing through the sausage meat. It is now ready to be stuffed into your meat of choice.

The revered 'Wellington' has long been feared by even the most proficient home cooks, when in fact it really is quite simple. There are a few key steps. Firstly, you must ensure you have seared the entire piece of meat in a seriously hot pan. You want this process to happen as quickly as possible to ensure you do not begin to cook the centre of the joint. The second key step is good pastry, rolled thinly. Finally, a scorchingly hot oven is all you need to give the pastry a lick of gold.

# Venison Wellington

— SERVES 3 —

### For the rough puff pastry
200g (7oz) cold grass-fed butter, diced
400g (14oz) stoneground unbleached white flour, plus extra for dusting
1 tablespoon fine salt
200ml (7fl oz) water

### For the Wellington
600g (1lb 5oz) venison saddle fillet
olive oil
1 garlic clove, finely chopped
200g (7oz) chestnut mushrooms, chopped
1 sprig of rosemary, chopped
80g (2¾oz) green lentils, cooked (we like Hodmedod's)
1 free-range and/or organic egg, plus 1 yolk, beaten

Start by making the pastry. In a mixing bowl, add the butter to the flour. Add the salt and slowly pour in the water. Gently mix together without breaking up the butter until you have a rough dough (it will feel quite dry). Wrap in parchment and chill in the fridge for 1 hour.

Remove the dough from the fridge and, using plenty of flour, roll it into a 1cm- (½in-)thick rectangle. Fold either end to the centre, then fold in half again. You should end up with something that looks a little like a book. Repeat the process again. This is called laminating. Chill the dough in the fridge for another hour.

Repeat the laminating with two more folds. Roll, fold, roll, fold. You should have folded the pastry four times in total. Chill the pastry in the fridge for another hour, and then it's ready to use.

To make the Wellington, generously season the venison. Add a little oil to a very hot pan, over a high heat, and brown the fillet until golden and just seared – this should take no more than 5 minutes. Remove the venison from the pan and leave to one side.

Preheat the oven to 220°C/425°F/gas mark 7.

In a separate pan, fry the garlic, mushrooms and chopped rosemary in a little oil until soft. Remove from heat and then add the cooked lentils and blend to a paste in a food processor.

Roll out the rough puff pastry until about 1cm (½in) thick. Spread a thin layer of the mushroom paste in the middle of the pastry. Top with the seared venison. Cover the outside of the venison with the remaining mushroom paste. Brush one side of the pastry with beaten egg, then fold the pastry over the top. You will end up with a strip down one side – simply press this down with a fork. Brush the entire parcel with beaten egg and cook for 10–15 minutes, or until golden brown.

Remove from the oven and leave to cool on a wire rack. Slice and serve with a dollop of horseradish sauce.

This is truly a sausage roll all dressed up for Christmas. Sweet, sticky fruit with the whiff of dark spirits in the background. We have made them fairly generous, but you could easily make them smaller and more dainty, to be eaten as a canapé alongside a schooner of sherry.

# Boozy Prune, Apple & Chestnut Sausage Rolls

— MAKES 6–8 —

75g (2¾oz) prunes, pitted and roughly chopped
2 tablespoons Somerset cider brandy
1 tablespoon olive oil
1 red onion, finely diced
100g (3½oz) fresh breadcrumbs
1 teaspoon freshly chopped thyme
1 teaspoon freshly chopped sage
½ tablespoon freshly chopped parsley
75g (2¾oz) cooked chestnuts, peeled and chopped
1 small apple
500g (1lb 2oz) sausage meat
500g (1lb 2oz) rough puff pastry (see page 270)
1 free-range and/or organic egg, beaten
pure sea salt and freshly ground black pepper

Preheat the oven to 220°C/425°F/gas mark 7 and line a baking tray with baking parchment.

Put the prunes in a small bowl with the cider brandy and leave them to plump up.

Meanwhile, warm the oil in a saucepan and cook the onion for 10–15 minutes until completely softened.

Tip the onion into a mixing bowl along with soaked prunes, breadcrumbs, herbs and chestnuts. Grate in the apple, skin and all. Crumble the sausage meat into the bowl. Season with salt and pepper and mix everything together well.

Dust a work surface with flour and roll out the pastry into a large rectangle about 3mm (⅛in) thick. Pack the sausage filling evenly along the pastry, lengthways. Brush one side of the pastry with beaten egg and fold over to make one large sausage roll. Press the pastry together where it meets using the tines of a fork and trim away any excess. Cut the roll into 6–8 even-sized portions and transfer them to the prepared baking tray.

Brush each sausage roll with beaten egg and bake for about 30 minutes, or until golden brown and cooked through. Serve warm, or chill them well and serve cold with a dollop of chutney.

A terrine is our secret weapon for surviving the festive season. It can be made ahead and brought out at a moment's notice. Fancy enough to impress, humble enough to satiate. Cut a slice or two, place on buttered sourdough toast and open a bottle of wine, and any guest will be happy.

# Ham Hock & Apricot Terrine

## — SERVES 10 —

2 x 1kg (2lb 4oz)
    gammon hocks
a handful of dried
    apricots, chopped
a handful of parsley
    leaves, freshly chopped
1 tablespoon wholegrain
    mustard
a good pinch of pure
    sea salt, to taste

Put the ham hocks in a deep saucepan, cover with water and set over a medium heat. Simmer for about 4 hours or until the meat is tender and falls off the bone.

Once cooled, remove the hocks from the water, reserving a little of the cooking liquor in a mug, and pick the meat away from the bone.

In a mixing bowl containing the picked ham hock, add the chopped apricots, parsley and wholegrain mustard and mix together thoroughly, adding a little of the cooking liquor. Season the mixture to taste with salt.

Line a terrine bowl or a loaf tin with clingfilm. Firmly push the ham hock mixture into the tin and cover with clingfilm, pressing everything tightly down so it is compacted. Refrigerate for 24 hours.

When you are ready to serve, remove from the fridge, give the tin a little knock and peel back the clingfilm. Invert on to a serving board or plate, slice and serve alongside some crusty sourdough bread and your favourite pickles.

A festive take on the much-loved Cornish pasty. Instead of letting the filling cook inside the pastry, this recipe involves braising the beef in the most delicious mulled wine first. Don't forget it is the chef's perk to enjoy a glass of mulled wine while you make these handsome pies.

# Braised Beef & Mulled Wine Festive Pasties

— MAKES 6 —

500g (1lb 2oz) rough puff pastry (see page 270)
1 free-range and/or organic egg, beaten

*For the filling*
2 tablespoons olive oil
1 onion, finely diced
1 celery stick, finely diced
1 carrot, finely diced
200g (7oz) swede, cut into 1cm (½in) cubes
1kg (2lb 4oz) grass-fed braising beef, diced
4 tablespoons stoneground unbleached white flour, plus extra for dusting
2 garlic cloves, finely chopped
1 teaspoon freshly chopped rosemary
2 bay leaves
½ cinnamon stick
1 star anise
4 cloves
400ml (14fl oz) red wine
2 tablespoons redcurrant jelly
150g (5½oz) cooked chestnuts, peeled and roughly chopped
pure sea salt and freshly ground black pepper

Heat 1 tablespoon of the oil in a large ovenproof casserole or saucepan. Add the onion, celery, carrot and swede and cook over a medium heat for 10 minutes until starting to soften.

While the veg is cooking, season the beef and toss it in the flour to coat. Remove the veg with a slotted spoon and set to one side. Now add the remaining tablespoon of oil to the pan and add the beef. Fry over a medium heat, stirring often, until nicely browned on all sides.

Add the vegetables back into the pan along with the garlic, rosemary, bay, cinnamon, star anise and cloves. Follow that with the red wine and redcurrant jelly. Use a wooden spoon to scrape and loosen any bits stuck to the base of the pan after browning the meat; it all adds flavour. Bring to a simmer and season with salt and pepper. Pop on a lid and slide it into the oven for 1½ hours, or until the meat is tender and the sauce is thick and glossy.

When the beef is ready, pick out the bay leaves, cinnamon and star anise. Taste and tweak the seasoning to your liking. Stir in the chestnuts and leave it to cool completely.

When you are ready to go, preheat the oven to 180°C/350°F/ gas mark 4.

Divide the dough and the beef filling into 6 equal portions. Dust a work surface with flour and roll out each ball of dough thinly. Use a plate (about 22cm/8½in in diameter) to cut each one into a perfect circle. Place some of the braised beef on one half, leaving a 1cm (½in) gap around the edge, and bring the other half over to make a semicircle. Crimp the edges together. If you want, you can use the pastry trimmings to fashion some festive decorations. Repeat until you have completed all 6 pasties. Sit them on a baking tray and brush with beaten egg.

Bake for 50 minutes, or until golden brown and piping hot.

There is nothing simpler, and more satisfying, than whacking all your gorgeous leftovers into a hearty pie. Throw in that leftover Christmas cheese, those last few shreds of festive ham, the drumsticks from the bird that never seem to get consumed at the same pace as the white meat – it can all go into the pot. This is not so much of a recipe, but more of a guide and reminder not to scrape your yuletide treats into the bin, but instead take a little time, a couple of pinches of this and that, and treat yourself to a memorable meal – again.

# Leftovers Christmas Pie

— SERVES 4 —

500g (1lb 2oz) rough puff
   pastry (see page 270)
1 free-range and/or organic
   egg, beaten

*For the filling*
200g (7oz) grass-fed butter
300g (10½oz) stoneground
   unbleached white flour
500ml (18fl oz) grass-fed milk
200g (7oz) clothbound
   Cheddar cheese (or any
   leftover Christmas cheese)
½ nutmeg, grated
300g (10½oz) Brussels sprouts,
   sliced (or any leftover veg)
200g (7oz) leftover Christmas
   ham, shredded (or use
   bacon lardons)
300g (10½oz) leftover
   Christmas turkey
pure sea salt and freshly
   ground black pepper

Preheat oven to 200°C/400°F/gas mark 6.

Melt the butter over a low–medium heat. Once completely melted, add the flour, beating it into the butter to make a paste. Gradually add the milk, whisking as you go, to make a luscious white sauce.

Grate the cheese and add to the white sauce along with the nutmeg. Add the veg, ham and turkey, along with a good pinch of salt and pepper. Pour the filling into a pie dish leaving enough room at the top for the pastry.

Dust a work surface with flour and roll out the pastry to 1cm (½in) thick. Lay the pastry over the top of the pie dish, then fork the edges down to seal. Add a couple of steam holes and use a pastry brush to brush the pastry with beaten egg – this will give it a golden finish once cooked.

Bake for 25–30 minutes or until golden brown.

# FARMING GLOSSARY

**Antibiotic resistance**
This is the reduction or total loss of effectiveness of antibiotics through repeated low-level exposure, which allows bacteria to evolve means of dodging their action. Historically, intensive farming systems have routinely fed livestock antibiotics to reduce death and disease prevalent in the unnatural, cramped conditions. While there are other causes of resistance, this is considered a major contributing factor in the loss of some of the most important antibiotics for human health.

**Artificial fertilizer**
A man-made compound of key plant nutrients made using chemical processes. The production process is no friend to the environment; the raw ingredients of phosphorus, potassium and sulphur are mined at a global scale while nitrogen is obtained in the form of ammonia through the incredibly carbon-hungry Haber–Bosch process. There are now many concerns about how these chemicals impact soil biology, and therefore the long-term sustainability of farms that rely on its use.

**Concentrate feed**
A scientifically formulated 'complete' feed designed to give livestock all the nutrition they need in every bite. This comes in the form of pellets called nuts or rolls, formulated by nutritionists from commodity-traded grains, and making use of manufacturing by-products, such as spent cooking oils or processing pomaces. More recently soya has also been piled into these, as its high protein content is particularly easy for animals to digest, making growth all the swifter. Such animal feeds drive deforestation to make way for soya, and contribute to biodiversity collapse by supporting the global grain commodity system.

**Forage**
This is a living, growing feed, but not grass, that the animal grazes direct where it grows. It is a useful tool in winter especially, when grass is no longer growing. Examples include kale (which was originally cattle feed, not a trendy cook's ingredient!), turnips and fodder beet, which is a carbohydrate-dense root vegetable. Sometimes the crop is harvested and fed direct.

**Grass-fed**
This can be a confusing term! It suggests the animal only eats a natural diet of grass rather than 'concentrate' feed (see above), but the legal definition of grass-fed allows for a proportion of the diet to be non-grass. 'Grass-finished' means the animal was fed concentrates from weaning. Only '100% grass-fed' means that is all the animal has ever eaten.

**Hybrid breed**
A bit of a confusing phrase, as all breeds are technically the product of hybridizing, but when discussing livestock this refers to a breed that has been developed for the purpose of increasing productivity of meat or milk above all else. It goes beyond natural cross-breeding, with genome sequencing, transgenic and cloning technologies involved in their production, driven by big business, patents and big bucks.

**Mixed farming**
A traditional style of farming where livestock are reared in rotation with crops, often cereals, for feed and bedding, as well as vegetable crops for human consumption. The manure from the animals creates natural soil fertility, avoiding or reducing the need to buy in artificial fertilizers.

**Mob grazing**
A system of improving livestock and pasture health by restricting cattle to relatively small areas of grass day-by-day using moveable electric fences, then leaving the pasture to recover for longer than normal, usually 40–100 days. This forces the livestock to eat more of the grass rather than picking off the tasty bits, which gives them better fibre and nutrition all while stimulating the grass to grow back stronger using fertility from the manure that is left behind and the extra time between grazings.

**Monoculture**
A crop consisting of a single species, which can be grains, pulses, vegetables, fibres or oilseeds to name a few. Such crops are typically grown at a large scale for efficiency at harvest, and usually involve the application of agrochemicals to keep pests and disease at bay. They are usually sold into the commodity markets, so provenance is irrelevant.

**Native breed**
A breed of livestock that has been developed over centuries of domestic farming to be adapted to suit a local set of conditions. This might be a sheep that thrives in wet lowlands such as Romney Marsh sheep, or hardy cattle like Galloways who can browse rough grasses and heathers of the high moors through tough winters but still produce excellent meat. There are over 160 native breeds in the UK, with animals bred to suit local conditions all over the world. These need protecting for their cultural and historic value, but just as crucially, as a local food system resource as there are some incredibly precious genes there.

**Silage**
This is grass or other green fodder such as maize, which has been preserved through fermentation for feeding to livestock in the winter season. It is stored either in large round bales wrapped in plastic, or in a 'clamp' on site at the farm - usually identifiable as a large pit or mound covered in plastic held in place by lots of old tyres.

## NOTES ON OUR CHEFS

This tome is a testament to the wonderful community that we are so fortunate to be a part of. It can be argued that the South West is the epicentre of the sustainable food movement in the UK, thanks to the many talented people who have put down roots here.

We are lucky that our friends happen to be some of the most talented chefs in the land, who have helped us to lovingly craft recipes that we hope will create memories for you and your loved ones to share for years to come.

### Abby Allen

Raised in rural Devon, where growing your own vegetables, catching brown trout in the river and picking out the Christmas goose from the fields of the neighbours farm was all part of normal life for Abby. Her passion for food and innate connection to the landscape where it comes from was instilled in her from a young age. Abby joined Pipers Farm over 10 years ago and during this time has built a deeper understanding of sustainable farming. Today she supports her partner Will in the running of Pipers Farm. Describing herself as a 'home cook', Abby is known for her love of gathering people together and feeding them! Included in this book are a handful of Abby's special family recipes, and tried and tested favourites that have been enjoyed around the kitchen table.

### Bob Andrew

Bob and Rachel go way back, having worked together at Riverford in Devon, where Bob was head chef at Riverford's award-winning Field Kitchen restaurant, and Rachel was in charge of the farm's communications. These days Bob has turned his culinary talents to recipes and new product development. His interest in sustainability was piqued in his mid-twenties on reading the quote from Wendell Berry: 'Eating is an agricultural act', which opened his eyes to field-to-fork eating. He spends his time at work cooking, writing and talking about food, and is passionate about encouraging people to eat seasonally and diversely. Outside of work, Bob can be found taking long walks on wild Dartmoor or making the most beautiful pottery in Rachel's scruffy barn.

### Connor Reed

We first met Connor when we were working with Hugh Fearnley-Whittingstall's River Cottage restaurants. Connor was an inquisitive sous chef who had a passion for wild food and sustainably reared meat. He subsequently became a cookery tutor at the River Cottage Cookery School where he worked with Abby, who by then was also working at River Cottage, and they became firm friends. This led him to join Pipers Farm where he trained as a butcher, learning from our incredible team, and once again he and Abby worked together to create recipes that celebrate seasonal, local food. Today, Connor works as a butcher in Paris. When not cooking or butchering, you'll find Connor exploring the countryside, foraging and wild camping. He is an advocate for real bread and is normally tinkering with his beloved sourdough starter, which rarely leaves his sight.

### Gill Meller

A man who needs no introduction! Our friend Gill, for those of you who have not yet discovered his talents, is an award-winning food writer behind a slew of bestselling cookery books. He has been a friend of the farm for many, many years, so many in fact, we cannot even recall when we first met! Over the years Gill has been a great supporter of Pipers Farm, championing our mission of rearing food in harmony with nature and supporting small-scale farmers.

Gill's own cookery journey started as a young lad, growing up in rural bliss surrounded by farmers, fishermen and wild food. His passion for food was nurtured by Hugh Fearnley-Whittingstall who placed Gill at the centre of his popular Channel 4 series *River Cottage*, and the rest, as they say, is history. Today, Gill is a food writer, author, food stylist and cookery teacher, living near the small fishing town of Lyme Regis, in Dorset with his family and two sheepdogs. When not in the kitchen Gill has a passion for his impressive vegetable garden, where putting his hands in the soil and nurturing his crops is a daily pleasure.

### Sam Lomas

Cheshire-born Sam started his career in cooking when he took on an apprenticeship at Hugh Fearnley-Whittingstall's River Cottage Cookery School, where he became good mates with Connor Reed and later met Abby. After leaving River Cottage, Sam moved out of the kitchen and did a short stint working for the Liberal Democrats! Realizing politics wasn't for him and hearing the call of the kitchen, Sam took up a position on the beautiful Isle of Anglesey to head up the Tide / Llanw Cafe at Halen Môn. Today, Sam is the head chef at Glebe House, a guesthouse, restaurant and 15-acre smallholding about 20 minutes from Pipers Farm in Colyton, East Devon. Sam is a serious talent, his visceral connection to food and understanding of seasonal ingredients won him a place on the television series *Great British Menu*, where he fought off tough competition to win the regional finals.

# INDEX

Page numbers in *italic* refer
to illustrations

## ACKNOWLEDGEMENTS

Without the vision, determination and sheer hard work of Peter and Henri, this book simply would not exist. Their unfaltering perseverance for over 30 years in creating a farming system that honours communities and respects the natural environment has inspired so many. It has also given us the most robust foundations from which to build a business that is deep-rooted in its values. Thank you for creating Pipers Farm.

To all our farmers, our sincerest thank you. Your dedication and commitment is astonishing. Thank you for providing the food that graces our plates and for leading the way in showing what good farming looks like. This book is for you.

Our wonderful Pipers Farm team, you are simply the best. Darren, our head butcher, your precision and expertise has set the standard for over 15 years. Garry, the legend of all sausages and burgers, what will we do when you retire! Duska and Henry, thank you for keeping everything running so smoothly. To all that have been a part of our journey and those of you who continue to take Pipers Farm forward, thank you for helping us make a difference.

Thank you to Matt Austin, our wonderful photographer and dear friend. Matt's magical photography creates a window into our world, allowing so many of you to enjoy our farm. Thank you also to Marie for making it all happen, for getting Matt to where he needs to be and dealing with all of our hectic schedules!

Connor, Sam, Bob and Gill, needless to say, we couldn't have done this without you. We are in awe of your talents.

Emma and Alex at Smith & Gilmour, thank you for bringing our idea to life, for your patience and expert knowledge, guiding us through making our first ever book.

Thank you to the team at Octopus, especially Jo, for wanting to make a book about a little farm in Devon. Because of you, we get to tell our story.

For Stan and Heather Hipkiss at Doggetsbeer Farm, Devon, who taught me the toil, joy and heartbreak of family farming in the 1980s. For Mum, Mary Rose, Ronald and Rookwood, who taught me how to cook and grow good food. For Guy Singh-Watson and Rachel Watson who taught me how to write about it. And for wonderful Violet and Bertie, for putting up with me banging on about this stuff all the time, and for caring about it as much as I do. **Rachel**

For Grampy, who instilled in me a love for rural life. Whose tomatoes will simply be the best I have ever eaten. Whose quiet, contented nature put every animal around him at ease. Who shaped me into the person I am today. Who sadly I lost during this project and will never get to see these words, but who knew how much I loved him and was so proud that I was making this book. **Abby**